OUTSIDE THE BOX

Published by Kudu Publishing

Cover design by Sara Young

ISBN: 978-1-959095-89-7 1 2 3 4 5 6 7 8 9 10

Printed in the United States of America

DR. BARTHOLOMEW ORR

OUTSIDE THE BOX

INNOVATIVE CHANGE FOR MORE EFFECTIVE MINISTRY

KUDU
PUBLISHING

This book is dedicated to everyone who wants to lead more effectively, leveraging innovation to change lives and make a difference in this world.

CONTENTS

Acknowledgments ... ix

Foreword ... xi

Preface ... xiii

INTRODUCTION ... 21

PART I. FOUNDATIONS OF CHANGE

CHAPTER 1. MESSAGE: BATTLING FAKE NEWS ... 31

CHAPTER 2. MATURITY: GROWING DEEPER AND GOING HIGHER ... 45

PART II. FORWARDING THE CHANGE

CHAPTER 3. MENTORING: BREAKING AND CREATING CYCLES ... 65

CHAPTER 4. MENTORING: KEEPING IT GOING ... 73

PART III. FEARLESS CHANGE

CHAPTER 5. MISSIONS: MAKING IT FULFILLING ... 87

CHAPTER 6. MISSIONS: MAKING IT FAR-REACHING ... 95

CHAPTER 7. MINISTRY: MAKING IT KNOWN ... 101

PART IV. FRUITFUL CHANGE

CHAPTER 8. MULTIPLY: MAXIMIZING THE MISSION ... 115

CHAPTER 9. MARVEL TOGETHER: POWERFUL CELEBRATION ... 125

CHAPTER 10. MONUMENTAL INNOVATION: LEADING INTO THE FUTURE ... 133

ACKNOWLEDGMENTS

I first want to give thanks to my Savior and Redeemer, Jesus Christ, for His continued grace in my life, strengthening me to fulfill His calling every day. And to my wonderful wife, Valarie, who has been a tender companion through many years of ministry together, as well as to my sons. I am so proud to be your Dad.

To my staff at Brown Baptist Church who work tirelessly behind the scenes, you make it a joy for me to lead and I am grateful to serve the Lord alongside you. To my church family at Brown, you have made pastoring one of the greatest experiences of my life and I am delighted to see Christ formed in you more and more.

To Dr. James L. Davis, thank you for being a friend to me and a co-laborer in ministry over the years and I pray for many years to come. To Jeremy Vencel, who helped craft the messaging of this book with care and excellence, thank you for your diligence.

Finally, to my readers, thank you for entrusting me to speak into your life through this book. May God's Spirit equip your mind, encourage your heart, and enable your hands to put into practice these insights and principles, all for God's glory—to change lives and make a difference!

FOREWORD

I have had the pleasure of serving with Dr. Bartholomew Orr over the past decade as a collaborator in ministry. He began his pastorate at Brown Missionary Baptist Church as a young man and has faithfully served there for more than thirty years, as well as with other ministries around the globe. Pastor Orr became the senior pastor from humble beginnings at nineteen years old with a congregation of only sixty-seven members. Through a commitment to innovation and embracing change, he has guided this church to a membership of over 13,000 people with far-reaching, generational and geographical impact. Not only does he speak of using all means of communication to share his Savior, but he also implements it in his ministry through ongoing digital and media outreach.

What I appreciate most about Pastor Orr are: his courage to challenge the status quo, the way he inspires people to become better leaders, his willingness to embrace new ideas, and the way he models loving affection for his wife, children, and grandchildren. We have spent many hours talking about our lives, God's Word, what the Lord is speaking to us, and the role of the church in our hurting world. I am blessed that he has included me in his world and been a dear friend to me.

What Pastor Orr addresses in *Outside the Box* reveals God's intention for His people and for local churches in our culture. He provides clear descriptions on how to make a long-lasting impact on our families, churches, and communities. While some solutions are simple, others require an outside-the-box perspective, especially given the dramatic changes we have witnessed in our culture. I particularly enjoy the way he speaks to pastors and leaders with helpful insights from his extensive experience as a seasoned leader. Leading change, sustaining it, and duplicating it are truly challenging endeavors. He and I have discussed this many times in both of our ministries. This book brings to light the components of being a successful change-maker within any ministry.

To the reader who picks up *Outside the Box*: prepare to be inspired, instructed, and challenged to lead others with greater aptitude, thoughtfulness, and fervor!

To my friend, Pastor Orr: thank you for writing this book to equip us to become better leaders in whatever roles the Lord has placed us. As you often say, our purpose is to change lives and make a difference! You've done it once again.

Serving you,
Dr. James L. Davis
Leadership Development International
Palm Beach Gardens, FL 33411
LDIServe.com

PREFACE

On March 16, 2020, like many others, I faced an unanticipated change of plans. As a church, we came face-to-face with the reality of not having in-person worship due to the novel coronavirus sweeping our country and the world. Since I took leadership of Brown Missionary Baptist Church over thirty years ago, we've always had church services and events throughout the week. We never canceled under any circumstance. This invisible yet deadly virus momentarily put this longstanding tradition on pause. As a leader, I was devastated. All the plans put in place for the year seemingly disappeared overnight.

I called the year 2020 our *Season to Lead*—the year we would do more to positively impact our community. I increased our missional efforts inside and outside the walls of the church, seeking to make a difference in a major way and get our church members on the move for missions. As an organization, we immediately assumed we would have to make drastic changes all around. Many religious leaders around the country recorded a 25 percent drop in giving; therefore, jobs and activities at churches would be suspended because of the unknown future impacts of COVID-19.

"God, why in the world would this happen to us? To Your church?" After the last service was completed on March 15, 2020, I headed home only to be bombarded with calls from some of my members who serve in the medical world. Their words devastated me. My optimism to quickly reopen our church doors waned, and reality began to sink in. This pandemic was going to be here for some time, and we needed a plan in place.

Where do we start? What do we do? I recalled again that this was our *Season to Lead*. Yet, at this time, I did not know what I would be leading. I am accustomed to preaching to a full room. My church culture involves people responding to me during the message. A typical week of my life was preaching at funerals on Saturday and leading worship services Saturday night and two services on Sunday morning. Afterward, since preaching is my passion, I would often preach an evening service at another church. Sprinkle in there, occasionally catching a plane to lead mission efforts in other countries. My mind told me that this busy schedule would quickly grind to a halt as I watched news outlets gravely discuss the nationwide shutdown.

Like many leaders, I had to think quickly. The members of my church looked to me for guidance and decisive action. Staff members and volunteers waited for me to respond and give direction as to what was next. Some of their livelihoods were at stake. Organizations where I served on the board of directors also looked to me to calm fears and help develop a path forward. Business leaders bracing for major losses and possible closure wanted to know if there was a way to be successful and profitable in this season.

On top of that, my own family had concerns. As a husband, father, and grandfather, I had to provide answers to quell fears. They wondered what we were going to do and how we would navigate through this season. I recall feeling wrecked when staring into the eyes of my grandkids who looked to me for assurance; they sensed something wasn't right. On top of that, my wife, Valerie, and I had so longed to take a sabbatical vacation. The plans were in place and the tickets and accommodations paid for. My promise to her, after arranging for the proper staff to be in place to cover my extended absence, was that we would get away to recharge and enjoy God's blessings together. This trip should have happened in 2018, but I stretched it out to 2020. Then the shutdown happened, and everything went on hold . . . again. You can imagine my regret! We were long overdue for this. And now, as reality sank in, I realized I had made a mistake by not acting sooner.

"Lord, why this, and why now?"

> **WHERE DO WE START? WHAT DO WE DO? I RECALLED AGAIN THAT THIS WAS OUR SEASON TO LEAD. YET, AT THIS TIME, I DID NOT KNOW WHAT I WOULD BE LEADING.**

I took the rest of that Sunday evening to pray, process, and plan. Preparing for the worst, I began thinking through everything—finances, staffing, current projects, future projects, staying on mission, assisting with people's mental and emotional health, and much more. The list seemed endless! I began to assess what was needed and what could be put on pause. Given that I led a staff of over one hundred individuals, my goal was clearly to keep everyone on the payroll. Our church is known for being open 24/7—there is something happening all the time. Organizations of all kinds utilized our facilities daily for meetings and activities. As with many other leaders at that time, I was forced to think creatively about how to reasonably maintain our normal flow.

Our church was one focused on missions, and we always served in the community. We outreached into schools, nursing homes, homeless shelters, prisons, and food banks. We had our hands in just about everything locally as well as many ministries nationally and internationally. It was our mission to be the hands and feet of Jesus. Anytime there was a need, we were eager to practice hospitality (Romans 12:13). To fulfill this calling, our church needed a plan moving forward to ensure our vibrancy for missions continued.

As the hours passed for me on the night of March 15, one of my favorite quotes from John Maxwell swirled in my mind: "Everything rises and falls on leadership."Prior to this pandemic, I thought I understood this and lived it out fully. I was a seasoned leader for my own tent and in ministries beyond. God created me to lead and, up to this point, graciously equipped me to do so effectively.

Being someone who grew up in a four-room shack with no running water, my ceiling for success was low. No one expected a poor boy from Mississippi to do anything extraordinary. But the Lord had something different for my life and used my mother, Lorene, to place a vision for the world on my heart. She always told me about how God was going to take me places, and one year, she gifted me with a globe. This was not the typical gift a kid wanted; a globe is nice as an add-on gift but not the primary focal point. Nevertheless, she encouraged me to dream big and to believe God for the impossible.

Part of this dream was realized as I stood before Brown Missionary Baptist Church at the tender age of eighteen to be considered to serve as the senior pastor. My age was working against me. Paul's charge to Timothy to not let anyone despise him because of his youth (1 Timothy 4:12) strengthened me, though. Being single was another strike against my candidacy. Despite all that, Brown Missionary Baptist Church installed me as pastor. The church only had sixty-six members, and many of them were family members. With God's help and blessing, and through the service of many people, under my leadership, Brown has grown to over thirteen thousand members. The congregation who trusted my leadership and poured into me played a big part in this.

Reflecting on these humble beginnings, I realized that the plans that needed to be put in place would not stem out of my own brilliance. It would be the power of God working in me (Ephesians 3:20). As a follower of Jesus Christ, I believe He can do exceedingly and abundantly above anything I can ever imagine. So I take no credit, nor do I boast in anything except Christ. Practically, swift action was necessary to continue to work out the plan God had for us. This plan would require the instinct to move quickly. It required intellect to process information effectively. The plan would also require innovation. Innovation was critical and continues to be necessary for leaders to lead in every season.

LET ME BE PERFECTLY HONEST WITH YOU—INNOVATION IS NOT MY STRONGEST TOOL.

Let me be perfectly honest with you—innovation is not my strongest tool. In the past few years, I stumbled across being innovative. Some people say the way I preach is innovative. I will utilize anything to make the gospel of Christ clear to listeners. For some, your introduction to who I am came from a viral video of the "Flying Preacher."[1]

The "Flying Preacher" idea came about in November 2018, surrounding our church's Christmas production. In this particular year, we had a device to "fly" angels in for the production. As I watched them rehearse this part, I thought of how it could fit into my coming sermon in which I would discuss the return of Jesus. My instincts led me to use the device that was already in the church to fly me in while asking the question, "Are you ready for Christ's return?" My team didn't think anything of it; it wasn't planned, and we did not expect it to go viral. By the end of that Sunday, the video clip had over a million views. Many people applauded and credited that idea to innovation. Was that innovative or just novel?

There is a difference between innovation and novelty. Many people in our society confuse the two. Although they are similar, the differences are evident. Novelty is something that is not scalable or unsustainable. Novelty is the latest fad that gains popularity and notoriety quickly and then disappears. Innovation, on the other hand, is something that breaks from current methods, makes an impact, and lasts for the long haul. It changes the course of how we live.

Many shows I watched growing up had innovation built into them. James Bond movies were action-packed; they also were filled with gadgets and technology that

1 "Mississippi Pastor Dubbed 'Flying Preacher' Glides Into Christmas Service," *YouTube*, November 28, 2018, news video, 1:07, https://www.youtube.com/watch?v=rTMTumgT4ws.

seemed to be before their time. Television shows like *Dick Tracy* cast vision for what could be. He used a watch that enabled him to communicate with people audibly and receive phone calls. Yes, this 1946 show highlighted the two-way wrist radio that was only utilized by law enforcement and not given to the general public. Now, that was innovation! This popular device is now used by many around the world. A great number of individuals use smartwatches to help them check messages, monitor their heart rate, and count how many steps they take in a day.

Although I am not the most innovative person, I realized that in order to get through this global pandemic, leadership alone would not be enough. We needed *innovative* leadership. As I met with my staff on Monday, March 16, 2020, innovation was on my mind. I asked several questions that challenged my team to think outside the box that we knew well and were comfortable using: "How can we continue to do what we do effectively? How can we continue to spread the message of Christ when no one is in the room? How can we reach the world if we cannot leave the country? How can we continue to serve despite the warnings to socially distance ourselves? How can we continue to lead our community with sensitivity during this uncertain time?"

I galvanized our team, and we created an aggressive plan to adjust our current system to meet the demands of each day. We changed the way we facilitated worship by catering to online viewers only. We created virtual mission opportunities. We developed new online methods to connect with our members. Our prayer ministry built a prayer line that gathered remotely six days a week because prayer was something everyone needed, especially during this time. As a staff, we intentionally called all our members every month as a touchpoint to see how we could serve them.

WITH GOD'S HELP AND INNOVATIVE LEADERSHIP, OUR CHURCH MADE IT THROUGH ONE OF THE MOST DIFFICULT TIMES IN HISTORY.

With God's help and innovative leadership, our church made it through one of the most difficult times in history. I believe innovative leadership is what will help us create better systems for churches, businesses, and other organizations, providing goods and services to communities around the world. Therefore, that is the focus of this book—showing how innovative leadership can help organizations thrive in our ever-changing society.

Innovation is critical to how we lead organizations. Some even describe innovation as the primary difference between thriving and dying systems. Scott Bales describes it in his book, *Innovation Wars,* as the intrinsic element to remain viable as a business.[2] I believe if we combine strong leadership with innovation, we will keep our organizations relevant now and in the future.

I believe Jesus gives us a look into His innovative leadership in the Bible to guide us in producing change and making lasting impacts along the way. *Out of the Box* is divided into four parts:

- Part 1 will focus on Foundations of Change, holding firmly to the essential message of Jesus while unwrapping how to develop maturity in His followers.
- Part 2 will dive into Forwarding the Change. Simply accumulating the wisdom and knowledge that God has poured into us without emptying ourselves into the lives of others leaves a less impactful, spiritually bloated leader. We are called to mentor others on their journeys of following Christ to multiply our impact.
- Part 3 will look at Fearless Change. Here we will explore how Jesus lived out a mission and that His calling now rests on members of His church to complete what He began through strategic ministry.
- Part 4 will discuss Fruitful Change. In this section, we will consider how selected ministries have successfully used innovation to reach their communities for Christ, locally and beyond. While enjoying the joys of those kingdom successes, there are yet more people to serve and communities

2 Scott Bales, *Innovation Wars: Driving Successful Corporate Innovation Programs* (New York, NY: Morgan James Publishing, 2019).

of people to reach with the gospel. Therefore, we wrap up by evaluating where current leadership and innovation are still needed in order to fulfill our calling as leaders in the church and in our communities.

Regardless of where you are on your leadership journey, prepare to get outside your box and make a greater impact for Christ!

REGARDLESS OF WHERE YOU ARE ON YOUR LEADERSHIP JOURNEY, PREPARE TO GET OUTSIDE YOUR BOX AND MAKE A GREATER IMPACT FOR CHRIST!

INTRODUCTION

Jesus traveled throughout the region of Galilee, teaching in the synagogues, and announcing the Good News about the Kingdom. And He healed every kind of disease and illness. News about Him spread as far as Syria, and people soon began bringing to Him all who were sick. And whatever their sickness or disease, or if they were demon possessed or epileptic or paralyzed—He healed them all.

—MATTHEW 4:23-24 (NLT)

Is there a solution to the pollution that is all around us? Is there an answer to the problems in our community—a fix for our broken society? I wonder if there is a real solution available for America. Think about it. From the borders to the corners, America has some serious issues. Many have already asked the question, "Who can solve these issues, and to whom do we turn for answers?" What is the answer, and who has the answer? Is it the police? Can they solve our problems? No, because it's going to take more than specialized weapons and crowd-control tactics to deal with America's issues. Is it the politicians? No, it's going to take more than policies to deal with the complex challenges of human hearts. Some would say the answer is our parents. Maybe if we got parenthood right in the home, everything else would fall into place. I don't believe that even the parents can do it alone.

I believe that it's going to take more than weapons that instill fear and make situations more tense or political policies that can inform but not inspire or empower. Philosophies can get people thinking but cannot move people to action. Philanthropists can even donate resources to organizations with hopes of changing circumstances, but many times, resources can't meet people's true needs or even reach those with the greatest needs. Is there a real answer to our family-wide, community-wide, and nationwide problems?

Who has the solution to America's issues? I believe that if we had pastors and leaders who were bold enough to think outside the box, brave enough to step outside the box, and big enough to work outside the box, we could make a lasting difference! We can revitalize our community, mobilize our citizens, evangelize the lost, utilize available resources, strengthen God's people, capitalize on the economy, and realize our dreams . . . but it's going to take courageous leaders leading differently. It's going to take everyone doing their part to invest in others' lives and make an impact.

I know you may be saying, "Pastor Orr, are you serious about that? Do you really think that making ourselves think and live outside the proverbial 'box' is the key?"

My answer is, "Yes."

I believe this wholeheartedly because 2 Chronicles 7:14 (NIV) says, "If my people who are called by My name will humble themselves and pray and seek my face and turn from their wicked ways, then I will hear from heaven, and I will forgive their sin and will heal their land."

Unimaginable restoration, rejuvenation, and revival are possible—with the right leadership and right mindset, working humbly under the authority of God. Strong and thoughtful leadership is vital to our future! Effective leaders will exemplify how to take the Word of God to and do the work of God in the world around us. It's time to get outside the box.

EFFECTIVE LEADERS WILL EXEMPLIFY HOW TO TAKE THE WORD OF GOD TO AND DO THE WORK OF GOD IN THE WORLD AROUND US. IT'S TIME TO GET OUTSIDE THE BOX.

I remember saying these words many years ago to my congregation in Southaven, Mississippi. Many people looked at me like I was crazy to think of doing things in a different way to impact the world. Some of my more seasoned members couldn't understand or rather accept the concept. It was like I was using auto-tune, like some performers in the music industry.

To say that the President of the United States, parents, and politicians did not have the answers to our problems offended many people. I understand the importance of all those individuals in our society. We need to have a leader in the White House to help direct and shape our country. The United States of America conveys strength and vibrancy when we have a leader who can rally other world leaders to work together and form alliances for the well-being of all people. We need other local, state, and national leaders who will make decisions in the best interest of our nation and not for personal gain.

The apostle Peter shares insight for us as it relates to governmental leadership:

> For the Lord's sake, submit to all human authority—whether the king as head of state or the officials he has appointed. For the king has sent them to punish those who do wrong and to honor those who do right. —1 Peter 2:13-14 (NLT)

Governmental leaders play important roles and are necessary. We owe them our prayers and involvement.

Parents are important as well. All of us, for good or for bad, have been shaped by parental figures. Parents typically have around eighteen years to cultivate the minds of their kids. Lessons on work ethic, decency, respect, and teamwork are some of the many important values taught in the home. Children also learn how to cook, manage money, and—I am hopeful—understand their family history. These are things I learned at home, and I am a stronger man because of them.

Biblically, parents have the holy task of discipling their children. One of my favorite passages about parenting in the Bible is found in Deuteronomy. Theologians call this section the Shema. This scriptural passage gives all who will follow the Lord an important reminder of the reality of there being only one God. It was a reminder to the Jewish people of this important truth and a warning not to follow the false gods created by the world. Tucked beside this divine charge was also a command to parents, an instruction that conveyed the important responsibility of parents teaching and modeling a life of faith to their kids.

> "Listen, O Israel! The LORD is our God, the LORD alone. And you must love the LORD your God with all your heart, all your soul, and all your strength. And you must commit yourselves wholeheartedly to these commands that I am giving you today. Repeat them again and again to your children. Talk about them when you are at home and when you are on the road, when you are going to bed and when you are getting up. Tie them to your hands and wear them on your forehead as reminders. Write them on the doorposts of your house and on your gates." — Deuteronomy 6:4-9 (NLT)

Parents are to be the primary source of godliness and training for their children, revealing to them how to become the person God wants them to be. Mothers, fathers, grandparents, and guardians play an integral role in a child's physical, emotional, and spiritual development.

Politicians are critical figures in our society. They work to find ways to govern the people in a way that represents them well. In America, the government was created to serve in the best interest of the people. Abraham Lincoln reminded the divided nation of this notion in the "Gettysburg Address" as he honored the soldiers who had lost their lives in the war. He asserted that "government of the people, by the people, for the people, shall not perish from the earth."[3]

Politicians have the difficult task of contemplating the interests of all who come under their jurisdiction and creating policies to provide liberty and justice for all. God talks clearly about the importance of rulers and authorities. He declares that they have been put in place by Him to fulfill His purposes. Paul speaks on this in Romans:

> Everyone must submit to governing authorities. For all authority comes from God, and those in positions of authority have been placed there by God. So anyone who rebels against authority is rebelling against what God has instituted, and they will be punished. For the authorities do not strike fear in people who are doing right, but in those who are doing wrong. Would you like to live without fear of the authorities? Do what is right, and they will honor you. The authorities are God's servants, sent for your good. But if you are doing wrong, of course you should be afraid, for they have the power to punish you. They are God's servants, sent for the very purpose of punishing those who do what is wrong. So you must submit to them, not only to avoid punishment, but also to keep a clear conscience. —Romans 13:1-5 (NLT)

In God's eyes, politicians play an important role in the well-being of a nation and should be honored with our respect and prayers.

All the roles mentioned are important but, by themselves, will not produce the depth of impact that our world truly needs. We have seen some incredible presidents, politicians, and leaders who challenged America to dream big and create change, yet they failed to bring the nation together to repair the deeper issues ailing our society. I believe the simple instructions Jesus introduced to us

3 "The Gettysburg Address," *Abraham Lincoln Online*, https://www.abrahamlincolnonline.org/lincoln/speeches/gettysburg.htm.

in the Gospels guide and empower us to utilize our multitude of gifts to change lives and make a resounding impact on our culture.

I believe that achieving such a powerful impact can boil down to these five things:

1) Message
2) Maturity
3) Mentoring
4) Mission
5) Ministry

THE MESSAGE OF CHRIST IS THE OPERATING SYSTEM FOR BELIEVERS TO LIVE BY, BUILDING FOR US A CHRIST-CENTERED WORLDVIEW, A BIBLICAL LENS THROUGH WHICH WE SEE THE WORLD.

The message of Christ is the operating system for believers to live by, building for us a Christ-centered worldview, a biblical lens through which we see the world. As we live out that message, others visibly observe Christ living within us. We embody the message of Jesus in our daily lives, taking intentional steps to grow personally in maturity—especially those of us who seek to lead others. Even more, God did not save us to live on an island by ourselves, isolating His message from others. Sharing the good news, teaching, encouraging, and doing acts of service in His name are vital in our attempts to "present everyone fully mature in Christ" (Colossians 1:28). We must help individuals to grow spiritually, so they can also share the message of Christ and be on mission as well.

When we properly mentor others, we grow the kingdom of God with followers who are mission-minded and who will develop others in the faith. Being on the move outside our own churches through missions facilitates God's ever-expanding kingdom to touch more lives. When the previous components are in place, our ministry will cause life-transforming, generation-impacting, and community-strengthening change in our neighborhoods and beyond. I cannot emphasize this enough! Spiritually developing this generation and the next keeps this cycle of God-glorifying change powerfully moving forward, impacting our communities for generations to come for the glory of God!

PART 1

FOUNDATIONS OF CHANGE

CHAPTER 1

MESSAGE: BATTLING FAKE NEWS

As was Paul's custom, he went to the synagogue service, and for three Sabbaths in a row he used the scriptures to reason with the people. He explained the prophecies and proved that the Messiah must suffer and rise from the dead. He said, "This Jesus I'm telling you about is the Messiah."
—ACTS 17:2-3

It's a bird! It's a plane! No, it's Fake News! Faster than Alexa, more powerful than a lying mouth, and able to leap tall buildings with a single tweet. Fake news has become Superman! Think about it! That term was popularized by President Donald Trump and is still used by many individuals and groups today. Whether it be misinformation or disinformation about a public topic or a private matter, we all witness the presence and impact of fake news. We all need to remember something important: fake news has been around for a long time and will persist long after us. Nevertheless, we recognize it, and we expose it!

I really wanted to understand fake news and what it was all about, so I Googled it. Wikipedia.com appeared with a description, but you can't believe everything on Wikipedia since it can be a whole lot of . . . fake news. Here's what Wikipedia said about fake news: It's a type of yellow journalism, propaganda that consists of deliberate misinformation or hoax spread via traditional print and broadcast news or online social media.[4] This false information is mainly distributed by social media but is periodically circulated through mainstream media. Fake news is written and published with the intent to mislead in order to damage an agency, entity, or person to gain financially or politically; often using sensationalist, dishonest or outright fabricated headlines to increase readership, online sharing and internet click revenue. It's all around us—fake news!

It's gotten so bad that people don't even know whom to believe and whom to trust. Here's the thing I want you to know: everything you hear comes with an agenda. This principle has been around for a long time. As a matter of fact, when you look at the New Testament and the message of the cross, fake news surrounded Jesus Christ. The religious leaders of His day would not have been able to have Him crucified if it weren't for fake news. Let me show you what I'm talking about. Matthew 26:59-61 states:

> The leading priest and the entire high council were trying to find witnesses who would lie about Jesus, so they could put him to death. But even though they found many who agreed to give a false witness, they could not use anyone's testimony. Finally, two men came forward who declared, "This Man said, I am able to destroy the temple of God and rebuild it in three days.'"

4 "Fake News" *Wikipedia*, https://en.wikipedia.org/wiki/Fake_news.

And they said to themselves, "Now we got him!" and they ran with that. But guess what? That was fake news! Yes, Jesus said that He would destroy the temple of God and rebuild it in three days, but He was not talking about the physical temple. He was talking about His own flesh and blood—His body. Yet they used fake news to get Him crucified.

After He was crucified and buried in the grave, He rose on the third day, early in the morning. Pay attention to the guards when you read this account. An earthquake happened, and the guards witnessed everything. Look what happened in Matthew 28:11-15 (NLT):

> As the women were on their way, some of the guards went into the city and told the leading priests what had happened. A meeting with the elders was called, and they decided to give the soldiers a large bribe. They told the soldiers, "You must say, 'Jesus' disciples came during the night while we were sleeping, and they stole His body.' If the governor hears about it, we'll stand up for you so you won't get in trouble." So the guards accepted the bribe and said what they were told to say. Their story spread widely among the Jews, and they still tell it today.

Fake news!

The guards told the religious leaders, "The ground started shaking. That stone rolled away. There were angels!" But that was not the narrative the authorities wanted told.

"No, we can't tell that one! But here's the story we want you to tell."

And they're still telling it! Oh, fake news!

Even in Acts 17, when Paul and Silas were in Thessalonica, we see them being affected by fake news! They were spreading the message of Jesus Christ and were hit with misleading information that caused a great disturbance in the entire city, forcing them to leave.

Friends, it is up to each one of us to be true to the message of Jesus Christ! I want you to know that we are up against fake news! People will lie to you, lie about you, and lie against you! Why? Because they have an agenda. Here it is: Paul and Silas were preaching the truth, yet the word got out that they were turning the world upside down, that they had come to cause confusion in Thessalonica.

They were, in fact, worshiping and talking about another king named Jesus, but the accusation against them was fake news! Jesus is not another king; He is THE King of Kings. He is THE Lord of Lords! That is the foundational message we wholeheartedly believe and which is the key to our lives and ministries. Since fake news is turning the world upside down, we must be clear and compassionate in our message about Christ to turn this world right-side up.

SINCE FAKE NEWS HAS TURNED THE WORLD UPSIDE DOWN, WE MUST BE PASSIONATE TO CLEAVE TO AND SHARE THE FOUNDATIONAL MESSAGE OF JESUS.

You've seen this unfold right before your eyes for years. Things are worse in America because of fake news! Consequently, we've gotten to the point now that people don't trust each other. And, to my dismay, people don't trust those in the church. Sometimes, it is because our message is not clear about who Jesus truly is, and we emphasize less important topics. Sometimes, it is about the failing character of people in the church. Sometimes, it is a result of untrue information about Christians. In a very real sense, we've lost credibility with the world, and that is partly on us! We've lost the simple, beautiful message of Christ!

Since fake news has turned the world upside down, we must be passionate to cleave to and share the foundational message of Jesus. We have to get really clear and compassionate with it. Some of Paul and Silas's greatest work was done amid dis- and misinformation. When we as leaders and as entire churches become passionate about the message, some people will do whatever they can to stop the Word of God, to stop the gospel of Jesus Christ, and to stop us from winning souls, changing lives, and making an impact. But whatever the push-back, we must push forward the gospel of Jesus with clarity and consistency to produce powerful change in our churches and communities.

How do we champion the foundational message of Jesus Christ? Here is what we need to be watchful for: fake news. First, we need to be watchful for the fake news about *redemption*. I call this *the salvation Jesus brings*. Consider Acts 17:3 again, and look at what Paul was trying to do: "He explained the prophecies and proved that the Messiah must suffer and rise from the dead." Guess what Paul focused on? He went back to the cross of Jesus Christ. He let his listeners know that Jesus Christ died on a cross, but it was necessary for Him to die to redeem, or purchase back, our sinful souls from eternal condemnation.

Can I tell you something? The original Roman cross was not beautiful. I know we put it in gold, we wear it around our necks, and we put it on our Bibles. But think about it—the cross is not beautiful, cute, or politically correct. The cross was bloody. It exemplified suffering and pain. We don't like pain. We like things comfortable and pain-free, yet they took Jesus and nailed Him to a cross. They put nails in His hands and spikes in His feet. He was pierced in His side, and a crown of thorns was pressed into His head. And as He was hanging on the cross, they stripped Him, gambled over His clothing, mocked Him, and ridiculed Him. He hung in shame in order to die for our sins. The cross was not beautiful. The cross was bloody.

Let me tell you something else about the cross. The cross is bold. It's bold because it reveals that the only way to get to the Father is through His one and only Son, who hung on the cross. If we are going to be saved, washed of our sins, and forgiven for the wrong we've done, the only way is through the cross of Jesus Christ. This message is our bedrock! Is it your bedrock, personally? Is it the foundation of your ministry?

First Corinthians 1:18 (NLT) says, "The message of the cross is foolish to those who are headed for destruction! But we who are being saved know it is the very power of God." It's like the old hymn "Nothing But the Blood" by Robert

Lowry: "What can wash away my sin? Nothing but the blood of Jesus. What can make me whole again? Nothing but the blood of Jesus."[5] The message of Christ's redemption is bold and powerful, and we must hold firmly to the whole of it.

THE MESSAGE OF CHRIST'S REDEMPTION IS BOLD AND POWERFUL, AND WE MUST HOLD FIRMLY TO THE WHOLE OF IT.

Why is this so important? Why make a big deal of this foundational message? Here's why: Fake news says that everybody is going to heaven. Fake news says that all roads lead to heaven, and if you're sincere, no matter who you are and what you believe in, you will end up in heaven one day. Some even suggest that you really don't have to believe anything. "Just be a good person, and the Big Man Upstairs will let you into heaven," some say. I'm sure that you've heard these fake news reports before.

Have you ever been a passenger in someone's vehicle and fallen asleep? This happened to me one time. I was comfortably enjoying some needed rest with my eyes comfortably shut, then awakened to realize that the driver was about to take us on a highway that led into the wrong state.

"Hold up, driver!" I exclaimed.

Oh, he was confident and sincere in his directional abilities but very mistaken! You can sincerely go in the wrong direction and not end up where you intended. We mustn't believe something just because others have preached a gospel and have gone as far as saying there is no hell. We have got to be mindful that there is a heaven, and there is a hell. Jesus said in John 14:6 (NKJV): "I am the way, the truth, and the life. No one comes to the Father except through Me." Let's be crystal clear about this! Salvation is in no other name but Jesus. Acts 4:12

5 Robert Lowry, "Nothing but the Blood," 1876, public domain.

(BSB) states, "There is no other name under heaven given to men by which we must be saved." Does your church believe this truth? Is this message evident in your ministry?

There is endless fake news about redemption. So, what is the Lord saying to us? The Lord is saying to us as leaders that we need to know and proclaim the truth. We need to present ourselves to God as one approved, "a worker who does not need to be ashamed and who correctly handles the word of truth" (2 Timothy 2:15, NIV). We need to take His Word and hide it in our hearts that we might not sin against Him. Like the psalmist wrote, I want to be "like a tree planted by the streams of water, yielding its fruit in season" (Psalm 1:3. NIV).

We need to know the truth. That's why we each have to read and know the Bible. We must meditate on and memorize scripture so that we may know these truths. Then when people bring us strange doctrines and spout their opinions, we won't go down that same road of destruction. Paul tells us in Ephesians 4:14-15 (NLT):

> Then we will no longer be immature like children. We won't be tossed and blown about by every wind of new teaching. We will not be influenced when people try to trick us with lies so clever, they sound like the truth. Instead, we will speak the truth in love, growing in every way more and more like Christ, who is the head of His body, the Church.

There is fake news about redemption. But you know the truth: Jesus Christ is the only pathway to get to glory. Salvation is not in Buddha. Salvation is not in Muhammad. Salvation is not in Eastern meditation or positive thinking. Salvation is only found in Jesus Christ.

Not only is there fake news about redemption, but as we get the message out, understand there's going to be fake news about *righteousness*. I call this *the standard Jesus demands.* Paul had it rough in Thessalonica. He was accused of upending order in the city. When officials couldn't find Paul, they tried to arrest his Christian friends. Why? They were trying to stop what Paul and Silas were doing out of jealousy.

These adversaries even used troublemakers to start a riot in the city. Oh, when people are jealous and envious, they will not stop at anything to damage you and your ministry. And yet the Word took hold there! The Word made a difference in the lives of the Thessalonians. Scripture says that some of the Jews who listened to Paul's message were persuaded and became followers of Jesus, along with some of the God-fearing Greek men and quite a few prominent women. What kind of change did it make in their lives?

To observe the kind of change it made, we read in 1 Thessalonians 1:6-7 (NLT):

> So you received the message with joy from the Holy Spirit in spite of the severe suffering it brought you. In this way, you imitated both us and the Lord. As a result, you have become an example to all the believers in Greece—throughout both Macedonia and Achaia.

I pray that God makes you, me, your church, and my church that kind of example—an example to the world of what righteousness and holiness are all about. Paul continued:

> And now the word of the Lord is ringing out from you to people everywhere, even beyond Macedonia and Achaia for wherever we go we find people telling us about your faith in God. We don't need to tell them about it, for they keep talking about the wonderful welcome you gave us and how you turned away from idols to serve the living and true God.
> —1 Thessalonians 1:8-9 (NLT)

This is the standard Jesus demands. You see, when we get saved, Jesus expects each one of us to live a sanctified, holy, righteous life. He is calling us not to blend in with the world or to live like the world but to live a holy, set-apart life. All of us ought to have a testimony like that. Yes, I've done some wrong. Yes, I've got some stuff in my past. You don't have to try and dig up dirt on me. I will go get the shovel myself. We all have dirt in our lives. But "if anyone is in Christ, he is a new creation. The old things has passed away; behold, the new has come" (2 Corinthians 5:17, ESV).

WHEN WE GET SAVED, JESUS EXPECTS EACH ONE OF US TO LIVE A SANCTIFIED, HOLY, RIGHTEOUS LIFE. HE IS CALLING US NOT TO BLEND IN WITH THE WORLD OR TO LIVE LIKE THE WORLD BUT TO LIVE A HOLY, SET-APART LIFE.

What a wonderful change has occurred in my life since Jesus came into my heart! I looked at my hands, and they looked new. I looked at my feet, and they did too. They danced a different dance. They walked in a different direction. Why? Because the Lord made a change in me. Jesus expects righteousness from His followers.

Too often, though, people espouse a dash of fake news to make you think that you can do whatever you want to do, live like you want to live, and get to heaven anyway. Why is that the case? Because sin is deceptive and temporarily profitable. Don't you know sin is good for the economy? It pays to keep people in bondage. That sounds odd, but it's true. If people just got saved and lived righteous lives, we would ultimately close prisons because no more people would need to be sent there. If spouses really lived in holiness, then divorce lawyers would have to find new work. Families would love better and stay together.

If people fully trusted the Lord with their resources and His provision, casinos would lose profits. I'm sure you can envision the wonderful changes in your family, church, and community if living a holy, God-honoring lifestyle became the great treasure of our hearts. "Be holy, because I am holy," God commands His people (1 Peter 1:16). Do you think your world would look different if this became a foundational expectation among Christ followers?

We must battle the fake news about righteousness because it creates confusion in people's minds and tries to keep people in sin. It tells you, "Everybody is right! Everything is right! There is no wrong. Whatever you feel is right."

I recently saw firsthand that sin is profitable. My wife and I went out together late one Friday to get something to eat. I suggested we drive downtown to one of our favorite restaurants. So, we drove down to Life Kitchen, and I couldn't believe my eyes. I knew people partied on Saturday nights, but we arrived that Friday night, bars were wide open, and people were standing out in the streets with drinks in their hands.

What really struck me was a group dressed in yellow shirts, pushing a cart up the middle of my lane of traffic. Dancing to the loud music with alcohol in hand, they wore shirts with their names on the back, obviously not ashamed and wanting you to know who they were. They walked down the streets, giving free entertainment to onlookers. There was one person toward the back of the group with the name "Grandma" on her shirt. I turned to my wife with a look of astonishment. Sin is profitable, whether it be for attention, validation, money, pleasure, or power. And you wonder why people keep walking down that empty road. Do they not know there is a better way?

We must not only know the truth about redemption and righteousness, but we also need all believers to live out the truth. Notice that Paul and Silas were able to persuade their listeners because they were living examples of having genuine faith in a resurrected Savior. Friends, are we imitators of Christ or imposters of Christ? Are we disciples of Christ or dressed-up devils? Are we truly saints of Christ or sinners who masquerade as such? We need to be faithful children of the Father! In short, we've got to live out the truth, putting it into practice humbly and consistently—in the home, in the church, in the office, on Sundays, and on Friday nights.

WE PREACH TO PERSUADE. WE TEACH TO PERSUADE. WE WITNESS TO PERSUADE. WE'RE TRYING TO WIN AS MANY SOULS AS POSSIBLE TO JESUS CHRIST.

Lastly, there is fake news about responsibility. What is the responsibility of followers of Jesus Christ when it comes to the message of the cross? Acts 17:4 (NLT) says, "Some of the Jews who listened were persuaded." We preach to persuade. We teach to persuade. We witness to persuade. We're trying to win as many souls as possible to Jesus Christ. Is your message simply to share information? Is it crafted to convince people of their need for a Savior? Are you trying to persuade others to follow Jesus and teach others to do the same? I call this *the sharing Jesus commanded.*

The Lord has called each one of us to speak on His behalf as ambassadors for Christ, imploring others to be reconciled to God (2 Corinthians 5:20). Do you sense the call of responsibility in those words? The urgency and intentionality to speak on God's behalf the message that Jesus shared with His disciples? Yet, the words themselves need power behind them. Jesus is recorded as saying, "But you will receive power when the Holy Spirit comes upon you. And you will be my witnesses telling people about me everywhere—in Jerusalem, throughout Judea, in Samaria, and to the ends of the earth" (Acts 1:8, NLT).

The guidance and power of the Holy Spirit are needed in our message. As I prepare to speak, I often pray, "Lord, work through my words and lead me to what You want me to share. Prepare hearts to receive this message. You alone produce the growth, and I will do my part to plant the seeds of truth." There is a responsibility laid on each one of us, and especially those of us who are leaders in the church, to deliver the message of Jesus persuasively through the power of the Spirit.

OUTSIDE THE BOX

(WE OUGHT TO BE OPEN TO SOMEONE ASKING US QUESTIONS AS WE ARE ASKING THEM QUESTIONS, SUCH AS: THEIR PURPOSE IN LIFE, WHERE THEY PLACE THEIR HOPE IN CHALLENGING TIMES, THEIR BELIEFS ABOUT JESUS, WHAT HAPPENS AFTER DEATH, AND HOW THEY CAME TO BELIEVE THOSE THINGS.)

Let's look at one more series of observations about how Paul communicated the message of Christ at Thessalonica. In Acts 17:2-3, Paul exemplifies four strategies that, I believe, are also meant for each one of us. First, he *reasoned with them*. For three Sabbath days, he went into the synagogue with a plan to discuss parts of the Old Testament with his Jewish listeners. Reason means to dialogue. It means to question and to answer according to *Thayer's Greek Lexicon*.[6] God is saying to each one of us that when it comes to the gospel of Jesus Christ, the message of Christ, we ought to have dialogue with individuals. We ought to be open to someone asking us questions as we are asking them questions, such as: their purpose in life, where they place their hope in challenging times, their beliefs about Jesus, what happens after death, and how they came to believe those things. Moreover, we should give them answers. While we may not know the answers to all their questions, we will genuinely seek out responses and circle back to them. We are reasoning with them.

Not only did Paul reason with them, but he also *explained to them*. He explained the prophecies of the coming Messiah. He fully opened the Scriptures, which is what explained means.[7] The Bible opens at our fingertips through various apps on our smartphones. We possess immediate access to God's Word that we can open and share with a few clicks. Make sure you are using the Word of God as your foundation of explanation and defense instead of your opinions

6 Strong's Greek: 1256. Διαλέγομαι (Dialegomai)—to Discuss, to Address, to Preach, https://biblehub.com/greek/1256.htm.

7 Strong's Greek: 1272. Διανοίγω (Dianoigó)—to Open up Completely, https://biblehub.com/greek/1272.htm.

or manmade ideas. Paul opened the Scriptures, and he explained the parts that were relevant to the discussion. Use it strategically based on the unique circumstances of the conversation.

Thirdly, he *proved it.* The word prove means that he laid the biblical evidence close beside or next to the facts to justify his claims about Jesus.[8] A plethora of prophecies in the Old Testament were fulfilled in the New Testament in the life and person of Jesus. With a culmination of evidence, Paul pointed his listeners in the direction of Jesus as the Messiah, the Anointed One, the Son of God sent from above. He was able to prove to them that Jesus was the coming One.

Not only did Paul prove it, but he also led them to confront the reality with a response. Too often, we present truth to others but fail to invite a response, a call to action—a call to answer, "Whom will you serve?" Providing people with an invitation to act on the message brings the decision right to their front door. We need to do this regularly, inside and outside the church walls.

Fourth, we see that Paul was intentional to *proclaim* it. We've got to proclaim the truth—say it, write it, announce it, tweet it, DM it, post it, or share it however we can. As opposed to how I grew up, limited to a fixed location with my thoughts, you and I can now be present in our shoes but send a message into cyberspace for everyone on the planet to read. On my social media profiles, I've uploaded the same picture: one on Instagram and one on Facebook. On both of my profiles is a graphic of John 3:16 in the shape of a cross. Is it easy to share a message on social media? Absolutely!

Are you using these tools more often to proclaim yourself or your faith in Jesus? That's touchy, I know! Remember that you hold influence with people that no one else can reach as well as you can. I believe using social media to convey the gospel of Jesus is a good use of these online platforms and redeems this powerful tool that God has entrusted to you. Be unique. Be strategic. Be creative in your message. But don't keep it to yourself, Friend! Let your faith go viral. Why not leave an impact and let the world know about Jesus Christ?

8 Strong's Greek: 3908. Παρατίθημι (Paratithémi)—to Place beside, to Set Before, https://biblehub.com/greek/3908.htm.

IF WE WANT TO SEE LASTING TRANSFORMATION, WE MUST NOT ONLY GET THE MESSAGE RIGHT OURSELVES. WE, AS FOLLOWERS OF JESUS, NEED TO GET IN THE WORKOUT ROOM AND BUILD SOME SPIRITUAL MUSCLE AND ENDURANCE.

An integral foundation of change is getting the message of Jesus right! It involves knowing the truth, living out the truth, and speaking the truth with conviction, urgency, and compassion. The truth is found in the Bible and doesn't need to be sugarcoated or watered down. Like Paul and Jesus, we need not strive to be politically correct. The essential message is that we and those we lead must hold firmly to this cornerstone truth: there is salvation in no other person and no other thing apart from Jesus Christ. He is more than a good person, prophet, or teacher. He is God from eternity past who came in human flesh to save sinful men and women. He lived a perfect life, was crucified and resurrected, and reigns as King of Kings forevermore! These foundational truths are the cornerstone to lasting change in a person, in a church, in a community, and in a nation. In a world of fake news, we know and proclaim the good news, a stark contrast and one alone that brings hope, healing, and change to this world.

If we want to see lasting transformation, we must not only get the message right ourselves. We, as followers of Jesus, need to get in the workout room and build some spiritual muscle and endurance.

CHAPTER 2

MATURITY: GROWING DEEPER AND GOING HIGHER

So we tell others about Christ, warning everyone and teaching everyone with all the wisdom God has given us. We want to present them to God, perfect in their relationship to Christ. That's why I work and struggle so hard, depending on Christ's mighty power that works within me.

—COLOSSIANS 1:28-29 (NLT)

Why is there so much chaos in our community? Why so much confrontation among coworkers and cold-heartedness in some congregations? Why in the world is there so much craziness in

Congress, confusion among our children, crises within many of our companies, and crime in our cities? Why is there still carousing in the church? Why is there cheating among spouses, combating within families, and unwed children having children? Why is there so much compromise among Christians, corruption among clergy, and conflict within our churches? I believe the answer is simply this: a lack of maturity.

All those issues I mentioned were not pertaining to the world or the unsaved people in the world. I was talking about followers of Jesus Christ. These problems exist among Christians simply because of a lack of maturity—spiritual maturity in the body of Christ. Let me show you what I'm talking about. *The New York Times* produced a report that stated 91 percent of members in the United States Congress profess to be "Christian."[9] However, do you see overwhelming cooperation in Washington, DC? There appear to be limited conversations and crossing of the political aisle.

One could say that politics supersedes a unified front in doing what is best for the country. I believe this is due to a lack of maturity—spiritual maturity, in particular. Haven't they read Psalm 133:1 (author paraphrase): "How good and pleasant it is for brothers and sisters to dwell together in unity"? When you think about the importance of coming together as a faith family, remember what Jesus prayed to the Father in John 17:23 (NIV): "I in them and you in me—so that they may be brought to complete unity. Then the world will know that you sent me."

UNITY AMONG CHRISTIANS PROCLAIMS A MESSAGE ABOUT JESUS AND HIS ABILITY TO UNITE PEOPLE OF VARYING PREFERENCES, BACKGROUNDS, AND AFFILIATIONS.

9 Jonah Engel Bromwich, "The New Congress Is 91% Christian. That's Barely Budged since 1961," *The New York Times*, 3 Jan. 2017, https://www.nytimes.com/2017/01/03/us/politics/congress-religion-christians.html.

There is a greater purpose to our unity than simply being nice to each other. Unity among Christians proclaims a message about Jesus and His ability to unite people of varying preferences, backgrounds, and affiliations. While achieving such a victory currently seems to be fantasy, with God, all things are possible! You and I, as leaders, must pray for, exemplify, teach, and advocate for God's people to look beyond our preferences when it comes to the most important priorities of life—obeying God's Word, loving Him thoroughly, and loving our neighbors practically. When there is spiritual maturity, there is holy cooperation, unity, and working side by side for the glory of God. This powerful expression of God's presence serves as a foundation for change personally and in our communities, and we must daily choose to make it a reality.

Someone may be thinking that I am oversimplifying this topic of maturity. No, I'm not really oversimplifying it. The problem is a lack of spiritual maturity among God's people that fuels countless issues. One of the prime signs of maturity that we find in the church involves the tongue. Just by listening for a while, you can discern how wise people are, how developed their faith is, and what is going through their minds. Out of the heart, the mouth speaks. Watch out! You don't know what you're going to get. Many people don't know when to speak up and when to use their common sense to shut up. And it's all wrapped up in our tongue.

The writer of Proverbs 17:28 (NLT) shared a gem of wisdom: "Even fools are thought wise when they keep silent; with their mouths shut they seem intelligent." Isn't that something? You can even look intelligent when you're not . . . if you have the common sense to just be quiet. Some wonder why they have so many problems in their homes. It's the tongue! People feel like they've always got to use it, but they don't!

"Those who control their tongue will have a long life; opening your mouth can ruin everything" (Proverbs 13:3, NLT). A lot of couples are constantly cooking up a batch of pain and hurt because they just don't know how and when to use their words. The truth is that all of us are susceptible. On the positive side, I also know that many people do control their tongue instead of letting it control them.

WE NEED TO UNDERSTAND MATURITY IS NOT AUTOMATIC; WE MUST MAKE CONSISTENT EFFORTS TO GROW.

Since maturity is not automatic with age, association, achievement, or announcement, we must all work to grow up! You likely know that just because you grow older does not mean that you grow wiser or more mature. There are some twenty-, thirty, and forty-year-olds who are still childish and immature. Even within the church, you have people that have been saved twenty, thirty, or forty years who have been caught up in the same dumb stuff for decades. Why is that? Maturity is not automatic with age.

Maturity is not automatic with association. Just because someone hangs around the church does not necessarily mean he or she is a mature disciple. "Well, I showed up, and we had a good time. I said my 'Amens' and clapped my hands!" That's fine, but just showing up on Sunday will not make you mature.

Maturity is not even automatic with achievement. Do you know anyone who is successful in leadership, whether in the church or business world? Certainly, they've achieved a lot, but we all realize that those with power and money don't always control their words or behavior in a Christ-honoring way.

How about based on their own announcement? How many times have we heard a young person say, "I'm grown! They can't tell me what to do! I do what I want to do"? Just announcing that you're grown doesn't make you grown. Ironically, when some say, "I'm grown," they are still living in somebody else's house. They're still eating somebody else's food and wearing clothes that somebody else bought, but have the nerve to say they are grown! My dad used to always say it like this: "The time you think you're grown, there's the door!" Saying we are mature doesn't amount to much. Our church and communities need us to live it out! There is power in that!

We need to understand maturity is not automatic; we must make consistent efforts to grow. That's what I love about the book of Colossians. Paul is writing to the Colossian Christians because the challenge with them is the same challenge we have today: how do we develop mature believers in Christ Jesus? In that day and time, false teaching had gotten into the church and was leading some away from biblical truth.

The same thing is happening now. People in the church are tossed to and fro by strange doctrines—some are very subtle—and Paul was writing to them that his goal was to present everyone fully mature in Christ Jesus (Colossians 1:28-29). Friend, that's our goal! That's why Paul wrote that he was preaching, teaching, and warning everybody. He was saying, "I'm working, and I'm struggling and depending on Christ's mighty power to work in me so that I might help grow up others."

Let's echo that mission for ourselves: "O, Lord, I want to grow up to increasingly become more like Jesus in all areas of my life, public and private! Use me today to encourage and strengthen others to mature." Every day, that ought to be the goal for each one of us. What can I do this week to mature even more in Christ Jesus?

How do I know when I'm spiritually grown? How can I have maturity in Christ? Let me give it to you. It's going to take some effort. One sign of maturity is receiving what the preacher says from God's Word! Mature people listen and ready themselves to do it!

First, you have got to work in the Word. If we hope to have a maturing faith in Jesus, we must take some definite steps to get scripture into us, internalizing and implementing the wisdom of God. I call this *the study of God's Word.* We cannot be spiritually mature if we don't know the Word of God. In Colossians 1:28, Paul writes, "I'm preaching to every man, warning every man and teaching every man. . . ." And what is the resource for his proclamation? He is using wisdom from God. Proverbs 2:6 (author paraphrase) says, "From the mouth of the Lord comes wisdom, knowledge, and understanding. . . ." He has given it to us here in the Word of God.

For maturity, there must be a consistent, systematic study of all of God's Word—the Bible. Is this book the source of your beliefs, directives, comfort, hope, and understanding? For the leaders of God's people, are you drawing regularly from the wisdom and instruction of God found in His Word? There is no power for true change apart from His truth, and all of God's people need to know this is a reality for you.

BUT AS LONG AS WE'VE SPOKEN THAT WORD OF TRUTH OUT OF LOVE AND IN HUMILITY, LET THE LORD WORK IN THAT PERSON AND LEAVE THE RESULTS TO HIM.

Consider the words and actions of people. They say that they want to become more mature in their faith, but they don't show up in Sunday School, Bible study, or small groups. They don't read the Word of God daily yet still hope to be mature. This is deluded thinking. If any of us are going to grow, there must be consistency in this essential discipline!

How regularly are you getting into the Word of God? Do you have a plan for when you're there? We shouldn't just open the Bible to a random page and say, "Okay, God. Give me a word!" Can God give you something meaningful like that? Yes, it's possible. Would He rather you build a system and structure to how you're reading the Word of God to better understand the context of verses and the whole message of a book? Absolutely! We need to make sure that we are rightly dividing the word of truth (2 Timothy 2:15) and studying all of God's Word.

We can't pick and choose what we want; instead, we have got to read everything between the front and back covers. Get to know the whole counsel of God from Genesis to Revelation. I want you to see the progression in Colossians 1:3-5 (NLT). Paul wrote:

> We always thank God, the Father of our Lord Jesus Christ, when we pray for you, because we have heard of your . . . [Their what?] . . . faith in Christ Jesus and your love for all of God's people . . . which come from your confident hope of what God has reserved for you. . . .

Now, how in the world did they get that hope? We read at the end of Colossians 1:5 (NLT) that it came from hearing "the truth of the Good News." Paul elaborated by reminding them that they heard the good news from Epaphras (their pastor). What did Paul pray for that church? "We ask God to give you complete knowledge of his will and to give you spiritual wisdom and understanding" (v. 9). The result? God would answer this prayer, and they would grow as they learned to know God better. Later in the chapter, we read, "But you must continue to believe this truth and stand firmly in it. Don't drift away from the assurance you received when you heard the Good News" (v. 23).

Your responsibility and my responsibility, like Paul's responsibility, boil down to what all Christians are called to do: learn God's Word, seek to understand it with its instructions and promises, and hold to it in every season of life, good or bad, until we reach glory! We then turn around and impress on others the need for this integral discipline. Paul echoes this calling to spiritual leaders by saying that his goal is to proclaim God's entire message to them (v. 25).

That's why I, as a pastor, we, as Christian leaders, and every disciple of Jesus should not sugarcoat God's truth. Granted, we can't make people happy every Sunday from the church pulpit or in individual conversations. Others will take offense at Jesus's words and leave unsettled. But as long as we've spoken that word of truth out of love and in humility, let the Lord work in that person and leave the results to Him. I find solace in remembering what Paul wrote: "I planted the seed, Apollos watered it, but God has been making it grow"

(1 Corinthians 3:6, NIV). Leave your acts of obedience that influence other people's hearts and minds to the Lord to develop.

Personally, I must preach the entire message that God unfolds to me from His Word. Every person needs to have the opportunity to hear His full truth! You and I are the messengers, and that holds a lot of weight with me. This is the reason why Paul said in Colossians 1:28 (author paraphrase) that "we preach, teach, and warn everybody." Recall what the Colossian Christians did with the Word: they heard the Word, they learned it, they were filled with the Word, and they believed the Word and stood firmly in it. Their pastors and leaders proclaimed the entire message to them, using it to teach, preach, and warn.

That's why I said you've got to work IN the Word, like working ingredients into dough until you cannot separate one ingredient from another. It all has been mixed thoroughly inside the dough. In the same way, the Word is placed in our minds, and we fold it in over and over, kneading in other scriptures and examples, revealing how it has changed us and built our faith as we've trusted these promises and instructions. We have worked in God's Word, and it's in there to stay!

A REGULAR DIET OF SCRIPTURAL TRUTHS WILL STRENGTHEN OUR FAITH, PRODUCE CONFIDENCE, INSTILL DIRECTION, AND YIELD HOPE.

This does not happen automatically. People are not going to learn it right away or understand it completely. What Paul was saying to each one of us is to be a student of the Word! Like physical maturity is a long, slow process, so it is with spiritual maturity. A regular diet of scriptural truths will strengthen our faith, produce confidence, instill direction, and yield hope.

The Word bears fruit in you by renewing your mind, just as the message of Jesus changed your life on the day you heard and understood the truth about God's wonderful grace. How can a young man keep his way pure? Psalms 119:9–11 (NIV) provides the answer: ". . . by living according to your word. I seek you with all my heart; do not let me stray from your commands. I have hidden your word in my heart that I might not sin against you." Do you believe that the Word will change you and your listeners—your desires, direction, boundaries, and priorities? Something wonderful happens when you embrace the Word of God; it has a way of pushing the other stuff out. Do you have a cursing issue? A lust issue? A discontentment issue? Get the Word of God in you and keep laying that down as a sacrifice to the Lord. He will undoubtedly change you from the inside out. Some change is gradual, requiring patience and grace as we progressively see more victory in those areas. What He has started, He will complete.

That is also why we come to church and spend time with God's people. We approach this table to get a balanced diet of listening to biblical preachers, kingdom-focused music, and godly people! Sadly, many Christians choose to avoid this spiritual buffet out of apathy, sin, or distraction. I once heard a pastor say to his congregation, "Show me your friends, and I'll show you your future." There's truth in that, isn't there?

What's the takeaway? We ourselves and those alongside us must guard our diet—there are many delicious options to choose from. Intentionally choose what you allow to enter your mind and how much of it goes in. You wonder why you're struggling lately with an area of sin or distraction. Why are you not hearing from God more clearly? Have your joy and peace taken a dive? Consider what you are permitting to enter your mind and fill your time. Even those seasoned in the faith can revert to bad habits, and yes, they will stunt our growth. Let's not be satisfied with the current depth of our own maturity in Christ. There is always a greater extent to which we can love and trust our Savior and devote other parts of our lives to becoming more Christlike. Maturity is for all of us, and it doesn't stop!

WE LIVE IN A PLACE OF VICTORY, A PLACE OF HONOR SEATED WITH CHRIST JESUS. HE HAS DONE THE WONDERFUL WORK WE COULD NOT DO.

Our calling involves not only working in the Word (reading it, studying, memorizing, meditating on, and rightly dividing it on a daily basis) but also a second component of deepening our maturity: working out the wrinkles. I call this *the struggles of our flesh*. Every one of us has a past, some dirt in our lives that others don't know about. Every one of us has some struggle, some issue, and some rough edges. After salvation and until the day I die, I must work out those wrinkles. The same goes for you. The same goes for every Christ follower before us. Sinfulness in people is nothing new. What is new, however, has been birthed by our gracious God, and that work He began is powerful and transformative!

Let's consider Paul's description of what the Lord has done for His children: "For he has rescued us from the dominion of darkness and brought us into the kingdom of the Son He loves, in whom we have redemption, the forgiveness of sins" (Colossians 1:13-14, NIV). No one can truthfully say that they haven't sinned. Our nature is to reject God's authority, even from a very young age. We all lived in the dominion of darkness for a time—some longer and some not so long.

Paul explains that we were once far away from God. We were His enemy, separated from Him by our evil thoughts and actions. Yet He reconciled us to Himself through the death of Christ in His physical body. As a result, we are brought into His presence holy and blameless. Now we can stand before Him without a single fault. What unearned kindness to us from a holy and good God! That's deep!

You may be thinking, *I've got several faults, even right now, so how can I stand before Him without any spot?* That is the beauty of justification, being declared innocent of any guilt! Because God took away our sins through the blood of

Jesus Christ and then attributed to us the purity and righteousness of Jesus, now when God looks at us, He doesn't see our sinful past. He doesn't see what we used to do. He sees the blood of His perfect Son covering us. I like how Dr. E. B. Hill said it: "This was us . . . all messed up. So now when God looks at us, He no longer sees the sin, but he sees us covered with the blood of Jesus. What church folk love to do is look underneath and remind you of what you use to do. You need to let them know, 'No! God has covered me.'"

Seeing ourselves as God sees us and truly trusting in His full cleansing of our sins, strengthens us to continue working out the wrinkles that still remain in our flesh. We live in a place of victory, a place of honor seated with Christ Jesus. He has done the wonderful work we could not do. Now it is our responsibility to "work hard to show the results of your salvation, obeying God with deep reverence and fear" (Philippians 2:12, NLT).

WHATEVER THE ISSUES OR THE HABITS THAT YOU HAVE, ALLOW THE WORD AND HIS SPIRIT TO MAKE CHANGES INSIDE YOU.

If a Christian or a church family is going to mature spiritually, there must be the continual yielding of their lives to be transformed into the image of Jesus Christ. There is no easy way around it. Being a disciple of Jesus is a call to surrender, to live for Him above all other affections, until the day we take our final breath. Jesus exemplified the right mindset of yielding to the Father when He prayed in the garden, "Nevertheless, not My will, but yours be done" (Luke 22:42, ESV). The results of such a prayer will intimidate some. Why? Well, God may lead you to let go of something that has been precious to you, to go somewhere you've never gone, to do something that may get you ridiculed or embarrassed. But isn't that what a servant does—obey His master? And so, maturing deepens as you and I continue to count ourselves as God's faithful servants, and not just servants, but beloved sons and daughters.

A regular practice of surrendering ourselves to God takes us places. "When I was a child, I spoke and thought and reasoned as a child. But when I grew up, I put away childish things" (1 Corinthians 13:11, NLT). What should I do then since I've been covered by the blood of Christ and have been forgiven? Should I continue in my sin? God forbid that if I am dead to sin, I should live any longer in the sin. If any man be in Christ Jesus, he is a new creature. Old things have passed away, and behold, all things have become brand new. There ought to be a change in our lives, and in the lives of our congregations. Do you sense that desire in yourself? Do you convey the call to maturity to the people in your care? May God grant us a spirit of surrender and a spirit of holiness. No matter what we were or what we used to do, we ought to be working out the wrinkles in our lives so His character is more clearly seen through us. As John the Baptist confessed, "He must increase, but I must decrease" (John 3:30, ESV).

In addition to the Word getting into us to produce change, God has supplied us with His supernatural power to fulfill our calling to live out His will. We need the Holy Spirit to empower this change. The apostle Paul wrote to the Colossian Christians, "He has told us about the love for others that the Holy Spirit has given you" (Colossians 1:8, NLT). How can we truly love one another? You and I know ourselves apart from Christ's power—our love for others will fail. But thank God for His Spirit! This passage says that the Holy Spirit will give us a love for our fellow man. Remember how the apostle Peter's love for Jesus failed several times before He was crucified. But over time, Peter learned to unconditionally love his Savior, as well as to love Gentiles who did not keep the Jewish law. There is a change of heart that only God's Spirit can initiate and work out in us. Today, have you yielded to the Holy Spirit and invited Him to work His power in you?

He also equips us to accomplish other Christian responsibilities besides loving others unconditionally. Paul reminded his young mentee, Timothy, about what else had changed: "For the Spirit God gave us does not make us timid, but gives us power, love and self-discipline" (2 Timothy 1:7, NIV). Do you lack the strength, the willpower, or the self-control to obey Him in some areas? Well, you've got the supernatural power of God inside you in that yielded position of your heart, empowering you to do what is too difficult to do on your own. "Be strong in the Lord and in the strength of His might" (Ephesians 6:10, ESV). The Holy Spirit is the true source of empowerment to become like Jesus, and we mustn't rush past Him in our busyness because we think that we've got it covered. We don't. We need Him.

In essence, what God is saying is, "Let me help you work out the wrinkles." Whatever the issues or the habits that you have, allow the Word and His Spirit to make changes inside you. Paul continues to encourage his readers to fight the good fight, a battle not against others but within their own beings. Paul confesses:

> For when I would do good, evil is always present with me, and I find that there is a war going on. I want to do the right thing, but I don't do it. I don't want to do the wrong thing, but I find myself doing it. —Romans 7:18-20 (author paraphrase)

There's a real war going on between our new spirit and our old flesh, one that we must fight daily. We can relate! Do we get weary? Yes! Do we let down our guard sometimes? Yes. But do we have the power to overcome fleshly desires and weaknesses? Yes! Praise be to God for His indescribable gift! The only question is whether or not we will plug into that supernatural power instead of relying on our own efforts to do what is right. Let's be a student of the Word, taking our spiritual sword as a soldier in war, without which we are defenseless against the attacks of the enemy. And let's allow God to transform us through the power of the Holy Spirit. To work out the wrinkles, you need God's Word and God's Spirit!

OUTSIDE THE BOX

IF YOU WANT TO LIVE A FRUITFUL LIFE, LIVE A HOLY LIFE AND ONE OF RELIANCE ON HIM. WALKING IN SUCH A WAY PLEASES THE LORD.

If we're going to be mature, we need to work up a win! I call this *the sign of our faith*. Colossians 1:9-14 and 28-29 (NLT) have become life verses for me. I sign these verses when I sign my name because they mean so much. Paul writes:

> So we have not stopped praying for you since we first heard about you. We ask God to give you complete knowledge of His will and to give you spiritual wisdom and understanding. Then the way you live will always honor and please the Lord, and your lives will produce every kind of good fruit. All the while, you will grow as you learn to know God better and better. We also pray that you will be strengthened with all His glorious power so you will have all the endurance and patience you need. May you be filled with joy, always thanking the Father. He has enabled you to share in the inheritance that belongs to His people, who live in the light.
>
> For He has rescued us from the kingdom of darkness and transferred us into the Kingdom of his dear Son, who purchased our freedom and forgave our sins. . . . [And because of that] we tell others about Christ, warning everyone and teaching everyone with all the wisdom God has given us. We want to present them to God, perfect in their relationship to Christ. That's why I work and struggle so hard, depending on Christ's mighty power that works within me.

How do we work up a win? What does that life look like? It's not just a good life He seeks; it's a godly life. There will be a whole lot of good-natured people in hell because they haven't received God's forgiveness through faith in Jesus.

Scripture calls us to live godly lives. It explains that if we are really going to be mature, we are going to live fruitful lives.

What's a fruitful life? A fruitful life consists of the deeds that we do, the attitudes we convey, and the words we speak. In other words, God expects us to treat people with compassion, fairness, and goodness. He expects us to serve one another, to honor others, and to do good for them as we have opportunity. Without hearing your words, how would someone perceive that you follow Jesus Christ? Isn't it through the behaviors you show? Consider my paraphrase of Jesus in Matthew 25, "I'm coming back, and I'm going to tell you that I was hungry and ask why you didn't feed Me. I was naked, and you didn't clothe Me. I was in jail but you didn't come visit Me. I was sick and you didn't pray for me. You're going to say to me, 'Lord, when did we fail to do these things?' When you failed to do it to the least of these people around you, you failed to do it to Me." If you want to live a fruitful life, it must be marked by good deeds.

Jesus explained that our behavior impacts others for His glory: "Let your light so shine before men that they may see your good works and glorify your Father in heaven" (Matthew 5:16, NKJV). They do not have to be great deeds of valor; they should simply reveal the character of Christ flowing out of you and from your church. With all that said, I'm certain that some may believe that good deeds are an end in themselves, that doing good for others earns God's approval. Whenever you do something good, don't do it for yourself. Don't do it for pats on the back. Don't do it for your name to be called out. Do it to point others to Jesus Christ! Bringing glory to Him is the end goal and should be the motivation for any goodness that flows from you. If you want to live a fruitful life, do good for others, even the smallest acts of service. If you want to live a fruitful life, live a holy life and one of reliance on Him. Walking in such a way pleases the Lord.

One of these days, every one of us is going to stand before the judgment seat of Christ. We will give an account of what we've done in this body, with our time, in private and in public. God is looking for maturity in His followers. He seeks our holiness. We must live a holy life because He calls us to pursue it. Get into the habit of praying, "Search me, Lord. If you find anything that shouldn't be here, enable me to lay it down and cling to You instead." "Search me, Lord. Strengthen me to hold my lying tongue." "Search me, Lord. I surrender my worrying to You." "Search me, Lord. I repent of that slanderous tongue." "Search me, Lord! I want to live a holy life and one that shows You to the world." He calls us to holy living. For without holiness, no man will see the Father (Hebrews 12:14). To live a fruitful life is to live a holy life and one full of good deeds.

TO LIVE A FRUITFUL LIFE IS TO LIVE A HOLY LIFE AND ONE FULL OF GOOD DEEDS.

Let's stop playing games with ourselves and remind our churches to take their faith more seriously. It's time for all of God's people to grow up. What kind of games do some Christians play? We play the game of "Uno." Too many times, it's just about selfishly pleasing our own desires, and we justify walking over others rather than building them up. Instead, we ought to practice the instruction in Philippians 2:5 (NKJV) when it says, "Let this mind be in you which was also in Christ Jesus. . . ." We think more of others and their eternal souls than we think of our own pleasure or comfort.

Or maybe we need to stop playing the "Trouble" game. Some people we know are masters at that game. They are troublemakers and trouble starters. They keep trouble going. These attitudes and actions have no place in the body of Christ or in our homes. The Lord will enable us to not always give others a piece of our minds. Rather than hold to resentment and keep trouble going in the family or on the job, we forgive and restore relationships as much as it depends on us.

We also need to stop playing the "Clueless" game. Some in the church live just like the world all week long and then walk into church clueless like, "What have I done? I wonder whom the preacher is talking about. That's not me!" One final game that the church must stop playing is the slanderous game of "Speak Out!" For many of us, the trouble will stop if we would just stop running our mouths. Where there is no wood, the fire goes out. When gossiping ceases, the Lord will bring restoration and unity. We, as Christ's holy people, need to stop playing these sinful games. Our calling in life is to live for the Lord, not to please ourselves.

It's time to stop playing games. Growing up is a foundation of change in our homes, churches, and communities. Without it, we lose all credibility, and the rest of our efforts becomes futile. Do your part to mature in your faith! Live like saints! Look more like Jesus! Love one another! Grow up in your living! Grow up in your giving! This world needs mature disciples. Our churches need maturing disciples to lead others.

I want to be like Jesus—who loved sacrificially, who walked in the power of the Holy Spirit, who obeyed His Father, and who set Himself apart to serve mankind at His own expense. Let's be like Jesus. Maturity is only going to start when we work in the Word, work out the wrinkles, and work up a win. All of these bring glory to Him.

PART 2

FORWARDING THE CHANGE

CHAPTER 3

MENTORING: BREAKING AND CREATING CYCLES

"Timothy, my dear son, be strong through the grace that God gives you in Christ Jesus. You have heard me teach things that have been confirmed by many reliable witnesses. Now teach these truths to other trustworthy people who will be able to pass them on to others."
—2 TIMOTHY 2:1-2 (NLT)

I don't believe in generational curses. Many have the idea that bad habits are automatically passed from one generation to the next. They believe that children are being punished for previous family members' sins. You may have heard someone say, "My daddy was a rolling stone." For those too young to understand that reference, it means he was a cheater, and, as a result, the child could follow in those footsteps. Not the soundest logic, right? People believe in generational curses, but I don't follow that. My reasoning stems from what we find in Ezekiel 18:1-4 (NLT). Look what the Lord said through the prophet Ezekiel,

> Then another message came to me from the Lord: "Why do you quote this proverb concerning the land of Israel: 'The parents have eaten sour grapes, but their children's mouths pucker at the taste'? As surely as I live, says the Sovereign LORD, you will not quote the proverb anymore in Israel. For all people are mine to judge—both parents and children alike. And this is my rule: The person who sins is the one who will die."

What the Lord was explaining to the Hebrews was that if somebody had done wrong, the punishment was not going to be passed on to other generations. Instead, He was going to deal with the one who had committed the sin.

(THE BREAKING OF NEGATIVE CYCLES AND SUBSEQUENT LIFE OF GROWTH, IMPACT, AND VICTORY FLOW OUT OF INTENTIONAL INVESTMENT, DISCIPLING, AND MENTORING OF OTHER INDIVIDUALS.)

So, while I don't believe in generational curses, I do believe in generational cycles. I do believe the reality that some bad habits keep getting repeated. Haven't you seen some negative habits or cycles in your family or those in your church? Perhaps it's the cycle of teenage pregnancy or pregnancy outside of marriage. Maybe it is the cycle of deadbeat dads, absent fathers, drug addiction, gambling, or pornography. There are even cycles of sexual promiscuity, homosexuality, lesbianism, drug abuse, poverty, ignorance, and inferiority complexes. I do believe that these cycles are sometimes repeated among families from generation to generation.

The big question that comes to mind is how to break these cycles. Why in the world do we keep repeating the same dumb patterns? For instance, why would a child who sees a family member abuse drugs and witnesses first-hand the destruction it brings still decide to walk that same destructive path? Why do we allow ungodly cycles to repeat? What can be done about them? Moreover, what is God's will for His people as it relates to building His kingdom here on earth? To fulfill His purposes for us individually and as a church, we must intentionally and strategically forward on the change that He has graciously worked inside us. If we don't, then healing stops with us. Handing down the truth stops with us. The victory stops with us. Not on our watch!

The breaking of negative cycles and subsequent life of growth, impact, and victory flow out of intentional investment, discipling, and mentoring of other individuals. I am convinced that mentoring is God's plan. Consider Jesus's ministry and how He taught and prepared His apostles with a message that changed the world. It involved teaching, correcting, and encouraging with lots of patience over three full years. The twelve young men that He chose to be nearest to Him did not likely have biblical degrees, excellent manners, clean backgrounds, or any idea how to change a nation. In truth, they would have had many unhealthy and misinformed cycles of behavior to undo and refine, not unlike us.

Just as Jesus spent vast amounts of time to develop this ragtag bunch, so we also need to be developed, and those we mentor will need it. Jesus capped off His earthly time with these chosen followers by charging them: "Go and make disciples of all nations" (Matthew 28:19, NIV). Did they have life all figured out at that point? No, but they knew the One who did well enough to head in the right direction. Jesus's mentoring was complete, even while they themselves still had to mature. Old patterns were broken; new wineskins were made. Thankfully, God still uses crooked sticks to draw straight lines.

A modern way of describing this type of life-on-life investment is *mentoring*—investing in the lives of other pastors and leaders, even those within our own families, to help them mature as disciples of Jesus and make them better leaders. God called us to pass the baton of our faith to the coming generations and to mentor our peers to strengthen one another. Proverbs 27:17 (NIV) affirms, "As iron sharpens iron, so one person sharpens another." There is a human truth that people can accomplish more together than apart. Spiritually, you can achieve greater impact yoked beside somebody than as a single plow in a field.

A GOOD TEACHER WILL TEACH YOU WHAT'S GOING TO BE ON THE TEST, HOW TO TAKE GOOD NOTES, HOW TO PREPARE FOR THE TEST, AND HOW TO ACE THE TEST.

Mentoring is about keeping the cycle of success going. I really like how author and speaker John Maxwell explains it. He quotes leadership guru Peter Drucker who said that success without a successor is failure.[10] Keeping all of God's Word and wisdom—along with your experience—bottled up inside you successfully ends the propagation of all that was entrusted to you. This is not God's will. A good teacher will teach you what's going to be on the test, how to take good notes, how to prepare for the test, and how to ace the test. This type of teaching encapsulates what mentoring is all about—preparing others to love and obey the voice of God in every way possible in a world of compromise and

10 John Maxwell, "Leaving a Legitimate Legacy," *John Maxwell*, 3 July 2013, https://www.johnmaxwell.com/blog/leaving-a-legitimate-legacy/.

sin. Not only will mentoring break cycles of sin, but it will also produce the impactful change the world needs!

WE CAN COMPARE IT TO THE MAIN POINT OF JESUS'S PARABLE OF THE TALENTS: USE THE AMOUNT THAT THE MASTER ENTRUSTED TO YOU, WHETHER A LITTLE OR MUCH.

Paul clearly understood the value of mentorship. Look at his relationship and communication with Timothy, his "true son in the faith" (1 Timothy 1:2). Paul had taken Timothy along on his third missionary journey, investing time, wisdom, instruction, and his own life into the young man. As a matter of fact, Paul mentored other individuals throughout the pages of the New Testament letters too. What did Paul do to mentor these individuals? He details part of his method in Philippians 4:9 (NLT): "Keep putting into practice all you've learned and received from me—everything you heard from me and saw me doing. Then the God of peace will be with you." Those whom the Lord has poured into have a responsibility to share those experiences and knowledge.

We can compare it to the main point of Jesus's parable of the talents: use the amount that the Master entrusted to you, whether a little or much. A faithful worker will work with whatever is given to increase the Master's profit. Paul was a great example of forwarding to others what God gave him. He was confident that he had received the Word, had matured in the ways of the kingdom, and was walking in truth. So, he could rightly say in 1 Corinthians 11:1 (author paraphrase), "Hey! Follow me as I follow Christ." Paul then surrounded himself with those ready to live out that same vision. He further explained his method of mentorship by stating, "We loved you so much that we shared with you not only God's Good News but our own lives, too" (1 Thessalonians 2:8, NLT).

OUTSIDE THE BOX

Investing in other Christ followers involves sharing more than just the Scriptures. It involves opening our lives to others—discussing struggles, sharing experiences together, praying for one another, talking about family and work, loving each other through failures, and celebrating victories. It is living life together to intentionally build God's kingdom in others. And guess what? The Jesus in you will naturally leave a sweet aroma on those around you. You first need to identify who is walking the same direction as you. Whom has the Lord brought into your circle who is ready to walk with you as you follow Jesus?

THE JESUS IN YOU WILL NATURALLY LEAVE A SWEET AROMA ON THOSE AROUND YOU.

Practically speaking, I believe there are "4 Ts" to mentoring. The first T is *truth—the transference of truth*. When you mentor someone, you take the wisdom and knowledge that was given to you, and you pass it on to other individuals. The responsibility falls on us leaders to learn the truth of God's Word—its promises, instructions, warnings, messages for the saved, messages for the lost, kingdom values, and much more. We must continue growing in knowledge and wisdom and godly character, especially if we ourselves are going to stay rooted in truth on our personal journey and expect others to follow our lead.

A second element is *trust*—building a *trusting relationship*. You already realize that a person cannot open up haphazardly to just anybody. Because one's life will be unfolded before another and personal information shared, mentorship must begin in a trusting environment with you first demonstrating integrity and confidentiality. On the other side of that coin, you must carefully assess another's character before divulging your own personal information. Creating a nonjudgmental, compassionate atmosphere for sharing is essential for revealing more intimate details that need to be discussed.

A third T in mentoring is *transparency—inviting another to look at the typically hidden areas of life*. A lot of us look good on Sundays, but will we let certain others hang around us when we're not within the church walls? Mentoring relationships permit others access to see and to hear the real you without hiding things. Vulnerability with a mentor can be intimidating—yet so freeing—as this openness allows light to shine in darker corners of our lives while receiving the support needed to confront those areas.

Influence is powerful. Much good results from strong and patient mentoring. But it is also dangerous when we do it wrong. Jesus makes a striking comparison in Matthew 18:6 (NLT) for those who lead others astray with their influence: "If you cause any of these little ones who trust in me to fall into sin it will be better for you to have a large millstone tied around your neck and be drowned in the depth of the sea." When God brings people into our lives for us to influence, take it seriously. There is no room for taking advantage of them or pointing them away from full allegiance to Jesus. May God help us to lead with purity and pass on Jesus Himself to them. We must be sure that we live for Christ above all other priorities inside and outside the church walls.

WHEN GOD BRINGS PEOPLE INTO OUR LIVES FOR US TO INFLUENCE, TAKE IT SERIOUSLY. . . . MAY GOD HELP US TO LEAD WITH PURITY AND PASS ON JESUS HIMSELF TO THEM.

Lastly, mentoring involves *time—investing time for trust to build and change to occur*. Mentoring with the same person doesn't last forever as seasons of life change, growth is achieved, and new friendships develop. It says that, for an amount of time, I commit to pouring into your life.

You can see that within those four parameters—truth, trust, transparency, and time—mentorship can't happen with just anybody. Paul instructs Timothy, "You have heard me teach things that have been confirmed by many reliable witnesses. Now teach these truths to other trustworthy people who will be able to pass them on to others" (2 Timothy 2:2, NIV). In this passage, the mentor is reminding the mentee to be selective in the ones he chooses to mentor, but he needs to keep the cycle of success going!

In the next chapter, I want to build on the foundations laid out above, providing additional clarity on how to successfully forward the change that God has entrusted to you: identifying a person to mentor, the central purpose of mentoring, how to shape that relationship to make it effective, and having realistic expectations when mentoring.

CHAPTER 4

MENTORING: KEEPING IT GOING

"Once again Jesus went out beside the sea. All the people came to Him, and He taught them there. As He was walking along, He saw Levi son of Alphaeus sitting at the tax booth. 'Follow Me,' He told him, and Levi got up and followed Him."
—MARK 2:13-14 (BSB)

Mentoring is God's idea. Jesus did it. Paul did it. And countless other Christian leaders through the centuries have made spiritual mentorship a priority in their ministries, making a profound generational impact across the nations. This practice involves sharing your life with another person. It allows him or her to have a clearer understanding of who you truly are, how you deal with stress, how you pray, when and how you spend quiet time with the Lord, how you lead others, how you trust the Lord with finances, and much more. Mentoring is keeping the cycle of success going. As leaders, you and I are called to this. It is the method God gave us to forward the change that He began.

We should dig a little deeper into how to select someone to mentor. This is what I call *the character element*. You understand already that we can preach, teach, and warn a whole room of people, but we can't mentor everybody. You can only mentor a few individuals with your limited time, so refine your search parameters to narrow the options.

When it comes to mentoring, we should look for a person who demonstrates a hunger to change, to become more than what he or she already is, or to be used by God. As a sidenote, I want to reiterate something: before you mentor someone, you must be a person of character yourself, a person of conviction, someone who can be an example to others. Does that mean you must be perfect with no flaws or hang-ups? No, it doesn't. But you are aware of them, confess them, and are actively growing in your personal holiness so that those shortcomings become less frequent and less powerful in you. Thank God that He uses broken vessels to still carry water!

As you recognize those whom God placed in your path, you are looking for someone with similar character and conviction, yet not necessarily someone who is just like you. Paul realized that he could not share himself with just anybody. Paul admitted to young Timothy, his "true son in the faith," that God had surrounded him with individuals that he wanted to pour his life into, and Timothy was one of those individuals. (See 1 Timothy 1:2.) Can you imagine the joy and sense of awe to be selected by the apostle Paul to carry on God's message and work? What a weight and privilege! I'm sure that Paul also felt that weight and privilege but in a different way, as one who had the responsibility to do the pouring.

Now Paul was acutely aware that you can't pass on to others what you don't possess yourself. You've got to be a person of godly character. I like what Paul said in 2 Timothy 2:2 (NLT): "You have heard me teach things that have been confirmed by many reliable witnesses." Paul didn't have to hide or explain away what he had previously said. He was confident that it was truthful—all of it. Many people heard his words and were touched by the character of Jesus through him. Then he instructed Timothy to choose other people of good character to carry the message of Christ. Without godly character in the mentor and in the one mentored, the content of what is shared is brought into question. Hence, it is vital to look for people of character.

What other qualities should we seek in someone to potentially mentor? One additional characteristic is a person's willingness to learn and grow. Some may be willing to receive information but do nothing with it. You want to identify people who are not only willing to learn but also willing to live it out. They ought to be willing to put in intentional effort to become a person of Christlike character, a person of righteousness and holiness. Can you identify someone like this in your sphere of influence right now? Furthermore, look for people who are willing to love and lead others. You want individuals who prove not just to be a sponge but also a watering can to nourish others.

AS YOU INVEST IN PEOPLE, THE GOAL IS NOT JUST TO INSTILL MORE KNOWLEDGE BUT TO HELP DEVELOP IN THEM THE CHARACTER OF CHRIST.

But even those who water may grudgingly do it, so assess if they wish to lead out of love for God and for others. The heart of a man and woman is key! That old saying rings true: "People don't care how much you know until they know how much you care." As you invest in people, the goal is not just to instill more knowledge but to help develop in them the character of Christ. Focus on the mind and the heart. Did Jesus love? Absolutely, like no one ever has before or after. In fact, this quality defines His disciples: "By this everyone will know that you are My disciples, if you love one another" (John 13:35, NIV). Seek those who demonstrate compassion and care for the souls of others. Leadership will flow naturally out of genuine love for people.

A word ought to be said about the dynamics of those in a mentorship relationship. These individuals do not need to become best friends, although deeper friendships often result from times of sharing, trusting, and caring. Some people you mentor may wholeheartedly embrace it; some may gradually shy away from it. While there are many people in your life, you need discernment about whom you agree to mentor. We discussed it earlier—you want someone you can trust and who has potential. Yet, many people you know may have all those qualities. Here is where we need some help outside ourselves.

I believe it is the work of the Holy Spirit to bring people together. Have you ever been around certain individuals, and suddenly, it just *clicked*? God uses divine encounters to bring people together for purposes higher than they perceive. A person may not be whom you would have chosen to mentor (or to mentor you), but you can't get around that special spiritual bond. Don't judge the book by its cover. He or she may be chronologically older or younger than you, dress differently, or live on the other side of town, but don't rule them out. "Man looks at the outward appearance, but the Lord looks at the heart" (1 Samuel 16:7, NKJV). We ought to ask the Lord to send certain people into our lives, so we can pass on truth and godly wisdom. I'll tell you this—it will not be who you expect! But be available and be ready when the Lord brings that person to you.

Let's add another layer to this mentorship topic—*the content element*. Consider what Paul instructed Timothy to pass on to reliable witnesses in 2 Timothy 2:2—"these truths." Hear this carefully: Don't just choose the right person; pass *the truth* on to the right person. In mentoring, you're not reproducing yourself. I don't need a bunch of Bartholomew Orrs running around. There are currently several of us, and the world can't handle any more. What your home, your church, and your community need is to see more of Christ, the hope of glory, in you. The true content or what it is we're passing on consists not of what I feel or think or simply my experiences. It consists of communicating the truth about Jesus Christ, the eternal Savior revealed in the Bible, whom we can clearly know from the Scriptures. He is the way, the truth, and the life who is becoming greater in us and, in turn, the One we seek to reproduce in the lives of other individuals.

In 1 Corinthians 11:1 (NLT), Paul says it this way: "You should imitate me, just as I imitate Christ." Paul invited the Christians in the city of Corinth, and in every place he went, to follow his lead as he followed Christ. The most important subject he proclaimed was "Jesus Christ and Him crucified" (1 Corinthians 2:2, NIV). It began with the simple message of the good news of Christ, the power of salvation to those who believe; then, it proceeded to communicate their new identity as God's adopted children and how to live in the power of the Holy Spirit, serving in the church, sharing their faith with others, and many more biblical doctrines and practices.

IF WE DEMONSTRATE AND DUPLICATE FALLING IN LOVE WITH JESUS AND ALIGNING OUR LIVES UNDER HIS LORDSHIP, THEN WE HAVE SUCCEEDED AT MENTORSHIP!

Don't miss this—the most important content we can convey is Jesus Himself and truth that is rooted in the Scriptures. If we demonstrate and duplicate falling in love with Jesus and aligning our lives under His Lordship, then we have succeeded at mentorship! There is a lifetime of learning how to walk obediently and intimately with Him, and a mentor should walk with others along that path. We are messengers who pass on these truths to others, ultimately helping to develop a heart of obedient love for the Savior.

(NONE OF US CAN LEAD OTHERS SPIRITUALLY WITHOUT GOD'S EMPOWERMENT AND DIRECTION THAT ARE FOUND AS WE HUMBLE OURSELVES IN HIS PRESENCE.)

A third component of mentorship is what I call *the chance element*. This speaks of the transparency needed to lead others as well as the uncertainty involved. Paul tells Timothy, "My dear son, be strong through the grace that God gives you in Christ Jesus" (2 Timothy 2:1, NLT). The aged mentor tells his student to be continuously, consistently—on a daily basis—strong in the grace that's been given by God through Jesus and not in his own power.

How many times have we tried to muscle through life in our own human power and gifts, according to our own wisdom and clever rationale? Too often, I'm sad to say. Paul reminds Timothy that a mentor needs all this divine strength and grace. Why can't we do it in our own strength? Are you doubting my abilities, Pastor? Truthfully, yes. None of us can lead others spiritually without God's empowering and direction that are found as we humble ourselves in His presence. We recognize that without His grace, we are inadequate to lead others well. Such a spirit enables us to confidently live a life of transparency. We look good at church, right? You're wearing your best and looking holy now. But how do we look when we leave here? How do we look when the lights go out? How do we look behind closed doors? Are we the right person who is living out our potential? We can only do it if we are doing it in the grace that comes from Jesus Christ.

You see, if you're trying to live holy in your own power and might, you can fool some people some of the time. You might even be good at it for a few days or weeks. I'm here to tell you that our sinful flesh is too tough for us to handle by ourselves. That's why we say in my church service every week, "Greater is He that is in me than he that is in the world. I can do all things through Christ who strengthens me." (See 1 John 4:4 and Philippians 4:13.) I believe we need all

His strength and grace so that we can live holy lives, being transparent in public and private, so that a whole congregation or the one person we are mentoring can see us still living for Jesus Christ. "Lord, keep me humble, seeing my need for You, Your grace, and Your wisdom. Strengthen me to live a transparent life before You so that I can lead a transparent life before others."

OUR CALLING IS A LIFETIME COMMITMENT TO JESUS CHRIST, AND WE WILL TAKE WITH US THOSE WHO WISH TO WALK THE SAME ROAD.

Something also needs to be said about the expectations we bring to the table on this topic of mentorship. Whenever you take a chance to mentor someone else, it's not going to always turn out the way you think. How many of you have poured your life into someone only for them to grow up and go in the opposite direction? Every father and mother would love to say every one of their children did everything they were told. No child is perfect, and every child will fail to meet our expectations at some point.

As you can imagine, this is also the reality of ministry that every leader faces. In 2 Timothy 1:15 (NLT), Paul writes, "As you know, everyone from the province of Asia has deserted me—even Phygelus and Hermogenes." We don't know what these two fellows did, but we see that Paul poured his life into some individuals, and these two men were significant enough to Paul to get publicly called out for their abandonment. He contrasted these two men with Onesiphorus, the only one mentioned who visited and encouraged the apostle during his imprisonment.

Paul recounted more heartbreaking news in telling Timothy that certain godless chatter led some astray from the faith and had spread like cancer, as in the case of Hymenaeus and Philetus (2 Timothy 2:16-18). Again, two other individuals, whom we know little about, spread false messages which acted like cancer within the city and undermined the faith of some. As you read Paul's account in subsequent chapters, a man named Demas deserted him because Demas loved the things of life more than the Savior, and Alexander the coppersmith did him much harm.

The truth is that you can choose certain people and pour your life into them, but they still may end up rejecting your hand of investment. You can raise up children and feed them for eighteen, twenty-four, or thirty years and give them a roof over their heads, clothes on their backs, and shoes on their feet. Yet they still go astray. You can help people, reach out to them, be nice and kind, and still get hurt by them. Nevertheless, what God commands of us is to take that chance and keep on pouring into their lives to expand God's kingdom. Imagine if Jesus or Paul stopped mentoring others because a few people rejected them. Our calling is a lifetime commitment to Jesus Christ, and we will take with us those who wish to walk the same road.

(IF YOU LIVE IN THE LIMITLESS POWER OF GOD THROUGH HIS SPIRIT, YOU WILL ENDURE THE HARSHEST MOMENTS, THE RUDEST COMMENTS, AND THE MOST UNFAIR AND UNJUST ACTS.)

In the winding road of life and leading others, we remember with confidence that we live with power—not ours but that of the Almighty. It's been said that a lion doesn't need to prove its power. It struts in confidence, holding its might in check until the moment it is needed. Similarly, Christ's followers rely on the might of Another. Every morning, when you wake up, declare, "Oh, Spirit of God, fall fresh on me. I need Your strength. I need Your power. I don't know what I'm going to face. I don't know what temptations I'm going to run across. I don't know who may offend me or hurt me, but with Your amazing grace, I can get through it all."

Choose to humbly live in the power that can only come through Jesus Christ. If you live in the limitless power of God through His Spirit, you will endure the harshest moments, the rudest comments, and the most unfair and unjust acts. Trusting in God's perfect presence and goodness will give you joy, no matter what. You will know at the end of the day that you've done your part and given your best. You've lived your day for Christ and honored Him, and now you can rest, knowing that He's caring for the things you can't control.

When it comes to mentoring, it's about time investment. It is putting in some time for the things that matter most: investments in eternity and helping to develop minds and souls. Think of your own life. Somebody took time to be with you. Can you think of somebody who was there for you when you were growing up, somebody who invested the time? Maybe it was your own parent. A friend's parent. A teacher at school. A Sunday school teacher. A deacon.

Thank God for those who took the time for each one of us! I believe that all of us who are saved got here because somebody took the time to tell us the good news of Jesus Christ, from His birth to His resurrection. Thank God for those that invested their time. Someone prayed for God's mercy on us. Thank God for those who took the time! They lived a life in front of us and modeled holiness to us.

MANY OF US ARE LIVING LIVES THAT WE NEVER THOUGHT WE WOULD LIVE. WE ARE DOING THINGS WE NEVER THOUGHT WE WOULD DO. NOW GOD IS SAYING THAT IT'S YOUR TIME FOR THAT NEXT STEP.

What God is saying to each one of us is, "It's your time now." God has blessed us and raised us up for such a time as this. Many of us are living lives that we never thought we would live. We are doing things we never thought we would do. Now God is saying that it's your time for that next step. It's your time to invest in somebody else. It's your time to help bring up somebody else. It's your time to train up the next generation. It's your time to make sure you are living holy before somebody, leading in the right direction. It's your time!

Today, I challenge you to open up! Open up your eyes and look for potential in others. Look for that boy or that girl. Let them know, "I've been there and done that. I can show you a better way. His name is Jesus, and His instructions are for your good." Then open up your heart in order to love them. Be willing to share your life and be vulnerable. "I'm going to open my heart, and I'm going to let you into my life. I'm going to let you ask me questions and help you on your journey." Then open up your mouth to speak truth.

When you're mentoring someone, you must be willing to tell him or her the truth. The Bible says it like this: "Wounds from a friend can be trusted, but an enemy multiplies kisses" (Proverbs 27:6, NIV). Friend, I would much rather have someone tell me a painful truth than a lie just to make me feel good. If you're going to mentor someone, you must be courageous enough to open your mouth and speak the truth if they're heading in the wrong direction. Then open up your life, so they can see the truth lived out in you. Open up your eyes, your heart, your mouth, and your life.

GOD IS SAYING, "I DIDN'T BRING YOU THIS FAR FOR YOU TO KEEP IT ALL TO YOURSELF."

Oh, let's break the cycle that leads to destructive ends. Let's create new cycles for God's kingdom! Reach out to that person at your job to show them how to live for Christ outside the church walls and what a good work ethic looks like! See that young couple that's married and needs a seasoned mentor to guide them through the highs and lows of marriage. Break the cycles of divorce, poverty, and ignorance. Mentor the next generation in your home, church, or local school. Seek out that neighbor, that couple, that one on Sunday morning who sits alone. There is potential all around you. God is saying, "I didn't bring you this far for you to keep it all to yourself." Break the cycle and create new cycles of discipline, self-control, Bible reading, service, compassion, rejoicing, fellowship, and faithfulness.

When Jesus comes back, I want to hear Him say, "Servant, well done! You made disciples. You warned others. You invested time. You poured your life into others. You helped train up somebody else." Sitting quietly in our seats is no longer an option. Forwarding the change is the responsibility of us all!

PART 3

FEARLESS CHANGE

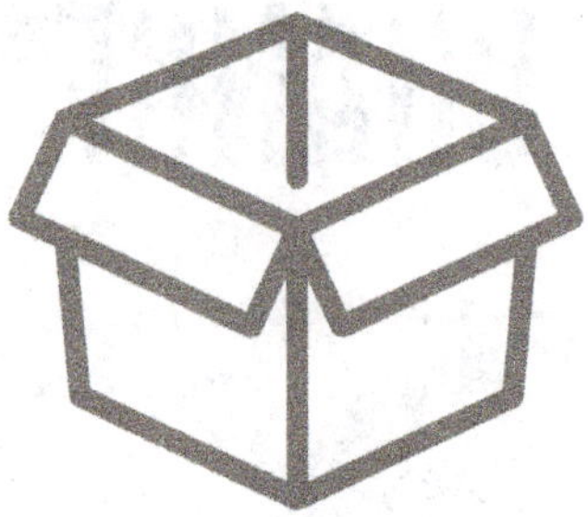

CHAPTER 5

MISSIONS: MAKING IT FULFILLING

"Among the prophets and teachers of the church at Antioch of Syria were Barnabas, Simeon (called 'the black man'), Lucius (from Cyrene), Manaen (the childhood companion of King Herod Antipas), and Saul. One day as these men were worshiping the Lord and fasting, the Holy Spirit said, 'Appoint Barnabas and Saul for the special work to which I have called them.' So after more fasting and prayer, the men laid their hands on them and sent them on their way".

—ACTS 13:1-3 (NLT)

What a church the Antioch of Syria church was! This group of Christ followers was a mission-minded, Spirit-filled church, birthed amid persecution and suffering. After the martyrdom of

Stephen in Jerusalem, we read that nearly all Christians were severely persecuted and scattered abroad, talking about Jesus wherever they went (Acts 8). Through these uprooted men, women, and children, the message about Jesus soon arrived in Antioch of Syria, just north of Israel. The church there was birthed during a time of struggle among an ungodly population. Antioch was a corrupt pagan city. Yet the Christian congregation was able to become firmly established and thrive, rising above prejudice, pettiness, hatred, and hostility. Antioch would soon become a church that would literally impact the world with the gospel of Jesus Christ.

At Brown Baptist, I often refer to the "6 Gs" that should define every church, the responsibilities of every local fellowship. We see these qualities demonstrated in the life of the Antioch church, and I believe they serve as guideposts to extending that which God entrusted to His people. Christ longs for His church to become healthy and stay vitalized, enabling her to be in a continual state of readiness to go on mission. Regardless of where that mission leads us, our posture remains the same—proceed obediently and fearlessly by faith with the life-changing message of the Savior.

Let me unpack these characteristics for you in hopes of casting a vision of God's intentions for His church and its mission. First, Antioch proved itself to be a *genuine* church. Look how the Bible describes it in Acts 11:21 (NLT): "The power of the Lord was with them and a large number of these Gentiles believed and turned to the Lord." When those traveling with the gospel arrived and proclaimed the truth in Antioch, genuine conversions took place. People were sure about their salvation!

GENUINE SALVATION PRODUCES FRUIT THAT IS EVIDENT FOR OTHERS TO SEE.

News of such rapid growth in the church traveled to Jerusalem, moving leaders to send Barnabas to investigate (v. 22). You can imagine that the people of Antioch were listening to the words of these visiting Christians, recognizing their lifestyles, conviction, and integrity, which gave credence to their message. The new believers started living out the truths of what they heard, learning to live as holy children of God. God's favor was upon them. Genuine salvation produces fruit that is evident for others to see. The church of Antioch became a light of God's presence, and the flame just kept getting bigger.

Notice that the writer of Acts describes Barnabas in Acts 11:24 (NLT) as "a good man, full of the Holy Spirit and strong in faith" who "encouraged the believers to stay true to the Lord" (v. 23). Through his godly character, generosity with his time, encouragement, and instruction, "many people were brought to the Lord" (v. 24). The power of one life is immeasurable! Life is about showing up and making our moments count! Barnabas's genuine faith and compassion left a lasting impact on the entire church. How much more impact could churches have on Sunday mornings and the rest of the week if we became like Barnabas (whose name means "son of encouragement") and committed to strengthening the faith of others? Genuine faith duplicates itself!

Not only was it genuine, but Antioch was a *growing* church. Acts 11:26 says that for a whole year, Barnabas and Saul (also known as Paul) stayed with the church, teaching large crowds of people. It was a growing church! Initially, when the gospel arrived, we read that many people came to faith in Christ. Large numbers were present, longing to be taught the truths about Jesus. They arrived to be fed spiritual meat and stayed for second and third portions!

While it is not said in this passage, it is possible that these Christians met very often together. The first-century church was described as meeting together daily to share meals, pray, learn the apostles' teaching, and fellowship (Acts 2:42). Not a bad recipe for growth! Multiplication is inevitable when Christians, whose lives match the faith they profess, genuinely love each other, walk in unity, learn God's Word, and seek Him in prayer.

Thirdly, Antioch was a *giving* church. Hearing that a great famine was coming to the entire Roman world, this church realized that there was a need for financial assistance among the Jerusalem believers. Together, they prepared and sent gifts to brothers and sisters in Judea whom they had never met, inviting Paul and Barnabas to deliver them. It was a giving church!

Some people may justify not giving to the Lord's work or to mission organizations by stating, "Giving is not my spiritual gift." But it doesn't have to be someone's spiritual gift to show practical compassion to others, especially to other believers. Money is just one aspect of giving. People need food. People need services done at their homes: repairs, grass to be mowed, and floors to be mopped. God's people need to be generous givers in whatever capacities they are capable of. "Therefore, whenever we have the opportunity, we should do good to everyone—especially to those in the family of faith" (Galatians 6:10, NLT). Giving should mark the lives of maturing individuals and churches.

Next, it was a *gifted* church. Antioch was filled with men and women who lived in the power of the Holy Spirit, sensitive to His leadings. We see in Acts 13:1-3 that prophets and teachers were present among the large group of believers and that there were fasting and praying. Scripture explains that every follower of Christ has been endowed with the Holy Spirit, whom we each desperately need for guidance, empowerment, and understanding. Sadly, many in the church do not use their gifts from the Spirit or rely on His wisdom and strength. We ignore and stifle what Jesus described as "the gift [the Father] promised" (Acts 1:4, NIV).

The Spirit does not force Himself on anyone; it is our choice to yield to him. "Since we are living by the Spirit, let us follow the Spirit's leading in every part of our lives" (Galatians 5:25, NLT). Each of us must choose at the beginning of the day and throughout the day to follow His leading. Otherwise, we rely on our human efforts, knowledge, and might to accomplish things that only the Spirit can do.

The presence of the Spirit always builds God's kingdom in and around us. One characteristic of a healthy church is Spirit-filled living that draws attention to Jesus Christ, not to us. The Antioch Christians used their gifts to strengthen the faith of others, and it thrived! God has given us gifts to use for the body of Christ. Every time we use these gifts, the church gets better equipped and encourages God's people. When one person decides not to share that gift, the whole body suffers.

(AS LEADERS, WE MUST CONTINUE TO CALL PEOPLE TO A HIGHER VISION. THEIR UNIQUE GIFTS MATTER, AND THEY PLAY AN IMPORTANT ROLE IN THE HEALTH OF THE WHOLE BODY.)

Paul elaborates on this truth in 1 Corinthians 12 when comparing the church and the gifts to a human body. Every part is essential to the full functioning of the body. Like Antioch, we are part of gifted churches. As leaders, we must continue to call people to a higher vision. Their unique gifts matter, and they play an important role in the health of the whole body. Their individual contribution may seem insignificant to them, but it is valuable in God's kingdom—the proclaimers, the cooks, the cleaners, the organizers, the servers, the worship leaders, the prayer warriors, the encouragers, the hands of healing—all are needed! All are essential to sustainable growth.

It was also a *graceful* church. Showing others grace involves much more than simply being nice. Anybody can smile and give a greeting. Being a gracious person begins deep within the heart, where sincere love for others is the root system. Every word, attitude, and action that blossoms out of those roots of love is full of grace. "We love because He first loved us" (1 John 4:19, NIV). What I like about the church at Antioch is that they were sweet to saints and sinners alike. Acts 13:23 tells us that when Barnabas got to the church in Antioch, he saw the evidence of God's blessing. Many people had already been brought to the Lord. One reason was that they knew how to treat one another.

Gracefulness is a fruit of God's presence in us. People like to be around others who show it. Being graceful says, "We may be different, but those differences are less important than our identity as children of God. My particular preferences are not my priority anymore; God's praise and purposes are my priorities." Think back to the recent spiritual awakening at Asbury University and in other locations across America. Certainly, each person there brings different worship preferences to their meetings. But you don't hear anyone complaining about the style of worship. Why not? Because their purpose for being there is to delight in Jesus, repent before Him, worship Him, proclaim His truth, and demonstrate care for each other. It was a beautiful thing to watch! May this spirit continue to spread across our campuses and churches! Being graceful begins with fixing our eyes and hearts on Jesus with an outflowing of sincere love for others. Is gracefulness a characteristic of your life and that of your church family?

A final distinguishing quality was that they were a *going* church. Acts 13:2-3 explains that they were worshiping and fasting, and the Holy Spirit revealed that Barnabas and Paul were to leave their church for a special work to which He called them. Notice that no one in that group tried to rationalize that it may not be easy to do, that it was not what was best for everyone else, or that it may affect the church's growing numbers. They continued to pray and fast, got together, laid hands on them in prayer, and then sent them on their way. The church supported the Spirit's calling. This was a going church!

How do you think the message of Jesus reached the ends of the earth? Did the apostles send letters to different countries explaining the gospel and then simply pray for their conversions? No. Jesus instructed His followers in Matthew 28:19 (NIV): "Go and make disciples of all nations" and to be ambassadors for Him, carrying His words with them. A going church recognizes God's calling to go—away from what is known and comfortable—and supports that calling with prayer and resources. The challenge falls in not attempting to intervene with human reason, which has deflated many Christians with visions of spreading the gospel. Antioch sensitively and fearlessly responded to God's leading, supporting and resourcing Barnabas and Paul to fulfill that calling. Little did any of them know the surpassing impact that this support would have on the known world!

Antioch became a going church for not just Paul's first missionary journey. He returned to report to his home church what God had done. Then they supported him on his second and third missionary journeys. Antioch literally became the sending church that had the most far-reaching impact for the name of Jesus. This was a church that was so fired up about missions that they did not mind sacrificing one of their leading teaching pastors for the gospel. Oh, for every church to be a going church!

THE WORK IS SO GREAT OUT THERE, SO WE MUST KEEP IT GOING IN HERE.

I sometimes hear the question in my church, "When are we going to slow down?" This is followed by my smile as I reply, "When we are done . . . Never!" The Lord has called us to go into all the world to preach and teach new believers the commands He gave while giving us confidence with the knowledge that He is always with us, even unto the end of the world (Matthew 28:20). I believe the promises and the protection of Jesus Christ are tied to us being obedient in going forth to make disciples for Jesus Christ. That's the reason I pray that my own church family and yours will continue to be a fearless church when it comes to mission work. The work is so great out there, so we must keep it going in here. Let's look at this together in the next chapter.

CHAPTER 6

MISSIONS: MAKING IT FAR-REACHING

"The Lord is not slow in keeping His promise as some understand slowness, but is patient with you, not wanting anyone to perish but everyone to come to repentance."
—2 PETER 3:9 (BSB)

There are some things that we ought to do inside the church to prepare us for what God has called us to do outside the church. We must equip the church body inside the walls so that we can do the work of the church outside the walls. We will keep worshiping here so that we can be witnessing out there. We've got to stay fired up in the church, so we can burn for Jesus in the streets. It is small-minded to believe that God's work is only for a select group who meet inside the church walls. Yes, when we gather, it is the time and place to stoke the fire and become equipped. We come to be pepped up and prepared inside, so we can be passionate out there. Sunday mornings and other mid-week gatherings are the moments to be trained, schooled, and encouraged by other saints. But these times are not the end goal. They prepare us to go outside to live out God's mission for our world.

TIMES OF WORSHIP, TRAINING, AND ENCOURAGEMENT ARE NOT THE END GOAL. THEY PREPARE US TO GO OUTSIDE TO LIVE OUT GOD'S MISSION FOR OUR WORLD.

What He pours in, we must pour out. The work God does within us is meant to be far-reaching in its scope. Every church must follow the principle in 2 Corinthians 1:4 (NLT) where Paul wrote, "He comforts us in all our troubles so that we can comfort others." The blessings, wisdom, and comfort that He has entrusted to us do not belong just to us; they are intended to be a blessing to others. In short, we are blessed to be a blessing! The entire Bible instructs God's people to take His message to Jerusalem, Judea, Samaria, and the uttermost parts of the world; it is His heartbeat. He wishes none would "perish but everyone to come to repentance" (2 Peter 3:9, BSB). Churches and individuals must not ignore these clear instructions.

For God's mission to the world to continue expanding, we each can take three actions. First, we keep praying for focus. I call this *the need for the right destination*. I believe a lot of churches are moving, but the problem is they are moving in the wrong direction. Often, we have an agenda, but it's not the Lord's agenda—our ideas of progress are not His ideas. We need to pray for clearer focus, beginning with, "Lord, not my will but Yours be done." One of the things I like about the church at Antioch is that they sought God for His will to be clarified and confirmed. Such prayers of earnest yielding before the Lord begin first with the leadership. Confess these prayers aloud for all to hear, so the people around you understand that your "Yes" is on the table, and the captain of your future is Almighty God.

Let us pray that God will give us focus for what He has called us to do in our communities and world. There is no shortage of opportunity, so we need the Lord to lead. One of the invitations we lay out at Brown Baptist is for our members to spend some time with the prayer ministry on Sundays and Saturday mornings before we serve. We also invite them to commit to praying at home. The Bible says that when these Antioch leaders came together to worship the Lord and seek His face, the Holy Spirit spoke clearly. After they fasted and prayed some more, they knew God's will.

LET US PRAY THAT GOD WILL GIVE US FOCUS FOR WHAT HE HAS CALLED US TO DO IN OUR COMMUNITIES AND WORLD.

The destination comes right from the Word of God. The way that we stay focused on this destination is by staying on our knees. Keep praying for focus. God calls us to simply follow the directions and trust His plan. Don't go to the right or left. We need to follow the directions that God has given to us in His Word and by His Spirit. God sent Paul and Barnabas on this first trip, then Paul and Silas on the second and third trips. Where is God leading you? Your church? To whom is God sending you? What work has He been leading you to do? Pray for focus; then follow the directions.

As you pray for focus, keep paying the funds. I call this *the dollars*. I said it before, and will say it again: the church at Antioch inspires me because it was a generous church:

> During this time some prophets traveled from Jerusalem to Antioch. One of them named Agabus stood up in one of the meetings and predicted by the Spirit that a great famine was coming upon the entire Roman world. (This was fulfilled during the reign of Claudius.) So the believers in Antioch decided to send relief to the brothers and sisters in Judea, everyone giving as much as they could. —Acts 11:27-29 (NLT)

How in the world is this church going to be able to keep sending Paul out on missionary journeys? I believe it is, in part, because some Christians in Antioch supported him financially for the cause of Christ. They willingly gave their resources as a seed of investment into the souls of those they would never meet on earth. If God has blessed us, He has blessed us to be a blessing to others. God has never asked us to give anything that He has not already given to us or will give to us. If God has not blessed you with many resources at this time, then you can't give much. Remember that He is looking for our willingness and faithfulness to obey His leading.

(LET'S STOP ASKING GOD TO LET OTHERS GIVE TO US. INSTEAD, ASK GOD TO PUT YOU IN A POSITION TO BE A BLESSING TO SOMEBODY ELSE.)

In the Antioch church, everybody gave as much as they were able to give because they recognized it all came from God. And if it all came from God, it all belongs to Him. So with the resources He has entrusted to me personally, I—by giving cheerfully to the Lord—am going to let Him move some around to use as He sees the need. Keep paying the funds for His glory!

I like to be on the giving end. Here's why: the only way you can be on the giving end is because you have something to give, and that is a blessing. Right now, you have enough and can help those in need. Later, they may have enough and can share with you when you need it. Consider 2 Corinthians 9:6-7 (NLT):

> A farmer who only plants a few seeds will get a small crop but the one who plants generously will get a generous crop. You must each decide in your hearts how much to give and don't give reluctantly or in response to pressure.

Paul completes that thought with an assurance: "And God is able to make all grace abound to you, so that in all things, at all times, having all that you need, you will abound in every good work" (v. 8). God has sufficient resources and knows the needs His people have. Let's stop asking God to let others give to us. Instead, ask God to put you in a position to be a blessing to somebody else. Let's be willing to share resources, so the work of God will reach beyond our own bank accounts.

TO BE MOST EFFECTIVE ON MISSION, WE MUST NOURISH OUR OWN SOULS IN HIS PRESENCE, WITH HIS PEOPLE, AND IN HIS WORD.

Third, we keep praising for favor. As the Antioch leaders worshiped the Lord and fasted, the Holy Spirit appointed Barnabas and Silas for the work to which He called them. It happened during their worship, their church service. Have you ever experienced that? All of a sudden, in the midst of praise and worship, the Holy Spirit shows up with a word, a confirmation, or a scripture? When we have decisions to make or questions that need answers, those are the times to worship, not worry. We come to get filled with the Holy Spirit, realigned with His will, and refueled to return to our local mission field. I call this *the devotion*.

OUTSIDE THE BOX

Praising at church is like coals nestling together to give strength and heat to one another, coming to get fired up, and to get our marching orders. When we praise God in spirit and in truth, no matter the circumstances, I believe the favor of God will show up. Oh, that our worship would be deep and true and honoring to the Almighty, and our hearts surrendered to His voice! May our churches live in this same spirit of expectation to hear from Him as we worship.

Yes, there is work to be done out there. Souls need to be saved out there. Homes need to be put back together out there. Marriages need to be strengthened out there. But let's remember that God is calling us to come inside, to get some healing, to receive some instruction and correction, and to be refreshed and refilled by the Spirit. This is not the time for division, to be separated from His church, or for bickering. Keep the fire burning on the inside. Keep reading His Word! Keep strengthening and encouraging brothers and sisters as you have the opportunity. Keep learning the truth and proclaiming it! Keep worshiping and fasting! To be most effective on mission, we must nourish our own souls in His presence, with His people, and in His Word.

CHAPTER 7

MINISTRY: MAKING IT KNOWN

"Jesus traveled throughout the region of Galilee, teaching in the synagogues and announcing the Good News about the Kingdom. And He healed every kind of disease and illness. News about Him spread as far as Syria, and people soon began bringing to Him all who were sick. And whatever their sickness or disease, or if they were demon possessed or epileptic or paralyzed—He healed them all. Large crowds followed Him wherever He went—people from Galilee, the Ten Towns, Jerusalem, from all over Judea, and from east of the Jordan River. . . .

"When He saw the crowds, He had compassion on them because they were confused and helpless, like sheep without a shepherd. He said to his disciples, 'The harvest is great, but the workers are few. So pray to the Lord who is in charge of the harvest, ask Him to send more workers into His fields.'"

—MATTHEW 4:23-25; 9:36-38 (NLT)

OUTSIDE THE BOX

A popular phrase attributed to Thomas Jefferson has circulated around the country in recent years: "If you want something you have never had, you must be willing to do something you have never done." Perhaps you have watched individuals, churches, and Christian organizations serve and gradually developed your own ideas of what would be most effective for your own ministry. And it works. It's good—not stellar—but it works. I wonder if the Lord wants to reveal more than what's always been done, more than what is realistic in our eyes, something richer, deeper, and impactful. Let's consider how Jesus did ministry. Before that, though, we should first look at what not to do.

THE LORD CHALLENGES US TO TAKE UP THE WORD AND A SHOVEL AND DO THE WORK OF MINISTRY OUTSIDE OF THE CHURCH WALLS.

In Isaiah 58 the Lord explained through the prophet to the Jewish people that they did worshipful deeds, but it was not His kind of worship. The passage describes how they fasted, dressed a certain way, and bowed their knees at times; however, going through those motions did not move God. Their widespread injustice, dissention, and exploitation took center stage before the Lord, negating their misguided acts of devotion. Churches need to beware of making certain things a main thing that shouldn't be a main thing and forgetting other things that should be a main thing. A problem arises when we sing, pray, and dance while the poor, widows, and orphans long for some compassion and assistance. Hungry people still need groceries. Is the church pursuing justice for the oppressed and speaking for hurting communities? In our freedom of worship, are we forgetting or ignoring the plight of those in need outside our church doors?

The Lord challenges us to take up the Word and a shovel and do the work of ministry outside of the church walls. That leads us to Jesus's words and actions in Matthew 4. I see several practical insights here to move us beyond what we view as acceptable ministry to outside the box ministry.

First, we see Jesus's *motivation*. "When He saw the crowds, He had compassion on them because they were confused and helpless" (Matthew 9:36, NLT). He looked around and saw not a crowd, but individuals—with names—who had deep spiritual and physical needs. They were like sheep without a shepherd. What moved Jesus? I believe it was His desire to bring wholeness and significance to each person. This speaks of His rich compassion for their eternal souls, weighted minds, and broken bodies.

Isn't that also where we find ourselves today? Our community is confused and helpless. They are weighted, worn down, and weary, despite their wealth. Even some of those with plenty of money take their own lives. They are emotionally exhausted, even after they've created a life of comfort for themselves. They are spiritually separated from God. Those people back then and today are lost sheep in need of a Shepherd to meet those God-shaped holes.

THE SAD THING ABOUT US TODAY IS THAT SOME OF US HAVE LOST OUR COMPASSION AND HEART FOR THE DOWNTRODDEN.

Without godly leadership, biblical morality, or heralds of the gospel of Jesus Christ, sheep will scatter and seek any available pasture to temporarily satisfy their undying hunger. We see this confusion and pain all around us every day. I believe that moved Jesus during His earthly ministry to take action, and it still does. The sad thing about us today is that some of us have lost our compassion and heart for the downtrodden.

Too often, we are more moved by songs than we are by lost souls or by the band but not by the brokenness around us. Why doesn't the church serve more in our schools, community centers, shelters, or local ministries? Could it be due to a lack of compassion? It is said that people make time for what is most important to them. Is showing practical compassion not a priority any longer? In whatever way we answer that, it is evident that Jesus is full of compassion and didn't shy from stepping into brokenness to bring wholeness. All ministry is birthed out of genuine compassion for others in need.

Second, I see the *mobilization* of Jesus. I call this *His concentration* because of where Jesus chose to work. Often, when churches begin thinking about ministry, they try to limit it to certain places or people. I don't see that in Jesus's life. The Bible said that He and His disciples traveled throughout the region of Galilee, Judea, and even Samaria. In other words, He was going from village to village and from city to city. Simply put, He was going everywhere. He didn't just stay in His own comfortable dugout, but He made it a priority to go where people needed His touch. He mobilized everywhere.

God wants to awaken us in our ways of thinking about ministry—we can't limit it to certain places. Too often, churches try to decide, "Are we going to be about the urban context or suburban, the inner city or the outskirts of the city, the city or the country, local or international?" To be honest, sometimes, people look down on others because some ministry is only international while others are all about the inner city. Can I tell you what God's version was? Go everywhere! Jesus is recorded in Acts1:8 (author paraphrase) as saying, "You're going to be witnesses unto me in Jerusalem, Judea, Samaria and to the uttermost parts of the world." That's exactly what His disciples did. They spread across what we know as northern Africa, to Spain and parts of Europe, all the way east to India. They got the message!

Should the apostles have disparaged one another for focusing on Asia Minor but not Rome or Syria instead of Athens? Not at all! Praise God for His call to certain places. Let's not judge where the Lord has led individuals and churches to minister but rather celebrate their specific focus, while we focus on where

God leads *us*. It may be in one or two areas or in a multitude of areas. But let there not be a restriction on where we are willing to go for Him. God wants us to go across the street and across the water. He wants us to go around the corner and up and down the highway. He wants us to go everywhere. Don't limit it according to the place.

(THE TRUTHS OF GOD IN THE BIBLE—INSTRUCTIONS, PROMISES, WARNINGS, ENCOURAGEMENT, WISDOM, AND ASSURANCES—ARE HIS METHODS TO RESTORE WHAT HAS BEEN BEATEN, BENT, AND BROKEN OVER THE YEARS.)

Sometimes, Christian mobilization limits itself to certain places; other times, it limits itself to certain kinds of people. We can't limit ministry to certain kinds of people or a certain demographic. Some prefer to serve a certain group, whether it's white or black, rich or poor, educated or ignorant, Gen Z or Gen X. Oh, I'm glad that Jesus didn't set parameters on whom He served! When it came to ministry, He served everybody.

Even when a Syrophoenician women, a Gentile, came to Him to explain her daughter was vexed with a demon, Jesus graciously chose to deliver the young girl (Mark 7:24-30). Why? His motivation was to show compassion and that His mobilization was everywhere and everybody! That tells me neither to look away nor limit God. It could be you or your church the Savior uses to reach a person, community, school, fire department, or entire region that no one has adequately served. We confess, "God, my, 'Yes!' is on the table. Where You send me, I'm willing to go. What You tell me, I'm willing to do." Let's mobilize like Jesus.

Third, we look at His *methods*. Throughout the Gospels, we read over and over that Jesus came to preach, teach, and heal. I call this *the complete cure*—service in not just one area, but all three. Herein lies the shortsightedness of our government leaders and even some church leaders. They advocate feeding stomachs and building houses but with no spiritual truth, or presenting the gospel without offering physical aid, or leading people to salvation without any discipleship teaching to mature them. It's all three, Friend!

Paul describes this concept of wholistic ministry in 1 Thessalonians 5:23 (NLT) "May your whole spirit and soul and body be kept blameless." I believe that preaching, teaching, and healing will serve each one of those—body, soul, and spirit. The body speaks of our physical lives, our flesh-and-blood tangible needs. God is concerned about the physical part of our beings. Recall that Jesus healed sick and broken bodies. He also was about feeding the hungry. It's hard to convince crowds that you are the Bread of Life when their stomachs are hungry. Ministry must not ignore this area while it cares for spiritual health. God compassionately restored many bodies and still does today within His divine plan. Such healing gives us a glimpse of our future resurrected bodies in glory when He will restore those broken places. Part of our methods must involve caring for people's tangible needs.

One ministry where the Lord led Brown Baptist to serve our community was in a nearby area that consists primarily of the working poor. We desire to make it possible for those who go to work every day to be able to go to a doctor when they are sick, as many can't afford insurance and don't get needed medical attention. We've decided to help pay some medical bills and make it possible for people to get tests done. Why? God is concerned about people's bodies and, therefore, so are we.

Paul also mentioned the health of the human soul. Rather than a ghostly, out-of-body reference, "soul" in this context speaks of your mind, your psyche, and your emotional well-being. The Lord desires people to experience mental and emotional well-being. How does He restore this internal part of mankind? He gives us teaching, the truth of God's Word. If you want peace of mind, stability in your emotions, or to change your perspective, those truths are available in the Scriptures. Do those in your church need this? How about those in your workplace, neighborhood, or your own home?

The truths of God in the Bible—instructions, promises, warnings, encouragement, wisdom, and assurances—are His methods to restore what has been beaten, bent, and broken over the years. Teaching these truths administers healing salve to our emotional and mental wounds. Let people know what He has said, and we will witness more people set free! "How can a young person stay pure? By obeying Your word" (Psalm 119:9, NLT).

How many of us have struggled? How many of us have ever gone through the valley and picked up the Word of God to read it? We are reminded that the Lord is our providing and protective shepherd, and we will not be in want. He makes us to lie down in nourishing green pastures and restores our souls. Wholistic ministry must involve teaching God's Word to others and patiently explaining how to integrate those truths in their lives, resulting in renewed minds and refreshed souls.

(WHOLISTIC MINISTRY MUST INVOLVE TEACHING GOD'S WORD TO OTHERS AND PATIENTLY EXPLAINING HOW TO INTEGRATE THOSE TRUTHS IN THEIR LIVES, RESULTING IN RENEWED MINDS AND REFRESHED SOULS.)

Not only for healing in the body and teaching for the mind, but God also gave us preaching for the spirit. While some may view the difference between teaching and preaching as just semantics, I refer to the spirit as that part of us that responds to God Almighty in relationship and preaching as the means of touching the spirit. Preaching helps connect us with God. Proclaiming the good news of Christ brings spiritual rebirth to a person, as Jesus instructed Nicodemus

(John 3:3). We proclaim that there is no other name by which men and women, boys and girls can be saved from eternal punishment for sins, except the name of Jesus. Let's make sure we preach the full gospel and get people saved. Each person longs for this but many are not yet aware of it, and God has called us to make them aware. This begins a person's journey of being alive spiritually.

The last observation from this passage involves what I call *the multitudes*. Matthew 4:25 says large crowds followed Jesus wherever He went—people from Galilee, from the Ten Towns, from Jerusalem, all over Judea, and from the east of the Jordan River. They were coming from everywhere. As a matter of fact, news about Him spread as far as Syria, and soon people began bringing to Him all who were sick. Whatever the sickness or disease, even if they were demon-possessed, epileptic, or paralyzed, He healed them all.

They were sheep—broken, lost, and confused—searching for a shepherd, a good one. And the crowds found Him. Would they find us just as ready to receive them, broken and dusty, looking for acknowledgment of their worth and healing for their whole beings? Often, we show up for ministry because we like being able to control the extent of it, but sometimes, ministry shows up at our door without notice. Is our response like that of our Savior?

Jesus looked out over the multitudes, was moved with compassion, and declared to His disciples that the harvest is plentiful but the laborers are few. Then He told them to ask the Father to send more workers to reap those fields (Matthew 9:37-38). Have you considered that you are the fulfillment of that prayer? That your church family, small group, or own family is the answer to the needs that others face? It is too much for any one person or church to handle. Each of us does a little . . . and much gets done.

Thank God for the crowds. They reveal that our hands, words, hearts, time, resources, and efforts are still desperately needed. Crowds remind us that the world is still broken and in need of wholistic healing in the name of Jesus. Crowds remind us that there is more to do. "Lord, what can I do to heal broken bodies, souls, and spirits in Your name?"

God wants a crowd. Consider the parable Jesus told of the man who threw a wedding feast, who told his servants to go inform all those previously invited that the preparations were ready at last. The servants returned empty-handed with some sad excuses from the guests. The master of the house pivoted, instructing the servants to quickly invite those in the streets, the poor, the blind, and the lame to enter the party and celebrate with him. Yet there was still more room in the house.

"Go out to the roads and country lanes to compel them to come in, so that my house will be full," was the instruction (Luke 14:23, NIV). Can I tell you something? God wants a crowd. He wants a crowd because He is not willing that any should perish but that all should come to repentance. The Lord wants a crowd. If we do what God has called us to do, I believe that not only will we go to the crowd, but also the crowd will come to us. As we lift up Jesus as the Source of all healing, He will draw all men to Himself.

OUR SELFISHNESS AND JUDGMENT KEEP US IN THE BOX WHILE GOD IS OUTSIDE OUR RELIGIOUS BOX WANTING TO BE INTRODUCED TO THESE PEOPLE.

And when the crowd comes to you, don't label the new people who are checking out what you have. We mustn't shun the lost just because they don't have it all together. Then again, do we? We can't say, "They're newcomers, and I don't like newcomers! They sit in my favorite seat and wear those street clothes!" No! Teach people to slide over and do the "sanctified scoot." Remind the holy rollers that they once were also "newcomers." Embrace the crowd because the Lord wants everybody to meet Him. Our selfishness and judgment keep us in the box while God is outside our religious box wanting to be introduced to these people. Until they meet Him, they are looking at you and your church family. We've got to get this right, or they won't be returning next week . . . or maybe ever.

GOD IS WAITING ON US TO ACT WITH THE RESOURCES AND GIFTS THAT WE HAVE—SMALL OR GREAT, OUT IN FRONT OR SERVING IN THE BACK.

When it comes to ministry, the church can't stay inside the four walls of the church. God is patiently, yet firmly, telling us to get outside the box, to reimagine what we view as realistic. A weakness that I see in churches is that we're only thinking about ourselves. While maturity in the church body and serving our own people are essential, some are only trying to help that group. Isn't it possible to demonstrate active faith inside and outside the church walls? God is waiting on us to act with the resources and gifts that we have—small or great, out in front or serving in the back. He is not done saving souls and providing healing. What can you offer Him to use? Following Jesus requires getting out the box. I pray that we will forever be a church that thinks beyond ourselves.

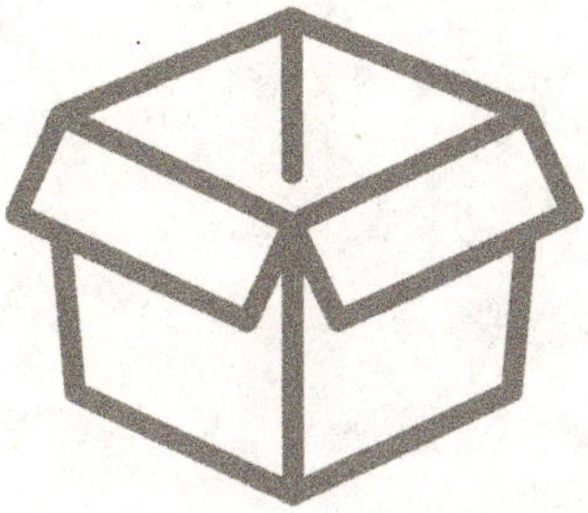

PART 4

FRUITFUL CHANGE

CHAPTER 8

MULTIPLY: MAXIMIZING THE MISSION

"And no one puts new wine into old wineskins. For the wine would burst the wineskins, and the wine and the skins would both be lost. New wine calls for new wineskins."
—MARK 2:22 (NLT)

The mission of the church never changes, but methods do.

We have seen how much the "church experience" has changed over the past twenty years, and it is simply amazing! People are different than they were twenty years ago—their attitudes, tolerances, expectations, previous experiences, and preferences. These silent filters remain in their minds as they consider attending a Sunday morning worship service for the first time—or the first time in a long time. There are mental and emotional filters in our communities that pastors and leaders today must recognize and confront.

A LEADER'S MISSION IS TO SHARE THE GOSPEL OF JESUS, DISCIPLE GOD'S PEOPLE, CARE FOR THE CHURCH, AND SERVE THE COMMUNITY; THESE ARE FOUNDATIONAL AND WILL NOT CHANGE. BUT THE METHODS WE USE MUST CHANGE FOR THE CHURCH TO CONTINUE BEING RELEVANT AND EFFECTIVE.

Pastors of years past would typically hold to a worship routine that had worked pretty well for decades. Yet, pastors of today must consider the cultural mentality of twenty-first-century Americans as they are preparing strategic communications and their ministries. A leader's mission is to share the gospel of Jesus, disciple God's people, care for the church, and serve the community; these are foundational and will not change. But the methods we use must change for the church to continue being relevant and effective. I want to unpack this in the following pages and share some innovative ideas that other churches have implemented to fulfill their missions.

Let's start with whom we're preaching to. As I mentioned before, the people sitting before us each week are not the same as a few decades ago. They have become increasingly accustomed to short soundbites of information, the use of personal stories to validate a topic, the comfort and efficiency of smartphones, digital communication, a slice of entertainment or fun from presenters, a customer mentality, opportunities to use or add to their social media feeds, and more. How are church leaders to stay true to their holy calling while dealing with these ever-growing conditions within the population?

As you know, things must change, or we lose people. That's the reality. Part of what I'd like to do here is invite you to consider what a guest sees, hears, and experiences when they do the following: pull into the church parking lot, approach the front door, enter the lobby, sit down in the auditorium/sanctuary, hear the music, meet the pastor, are invited to tithe, experience the closing, and leave the church. Additionally, the regular attendee needs consideration, given that the same cultural influences affect them also.

AS YOU HAVE INSIGHTS AND IDEAS FOR POTENTIAL CHANGES, REMEMBER THAT CHANGES ARE MOST SUCCESSFUL WHEN MADE GRADUALLY AND WITH A COALITION OF LEADERS.

Leaders must ponder each of these experiences as we think forward to not just this year but to one, five, and ten years from now. As you have insights and ideas for potential changes, remember that changes are most successful when made gradually and with a coalition of leaders. In the final chapter, I will describe some proven strategies to implement changes since arriving on Sunday morning and suddenly mandating a new policy to everyone may not go over well. For now, let's look at various areas of ministry and how some churches have carefully thought through these considerations.

DIGITAL MARKETING

People are used to learning about virtually anything through searching the internet, including churches. When looking at your church website, seekers (both Christians and non-Christians) will make a judgment about your church based on what they see and hear. Some churches have developed an introductory video message from the lead pastor on the homepage of the site. Be sure to highlight your vision and ways to serve those in the church and community. There are also high-quality photos of the worship experience that include the worship team, the pastor preaching, people being greeted, and other areas that pertain to each ministry. Because people want to get a quick snapshot of the church, they may decide to continue investigating your church from a quick perusal of that first webpage. Make that page count!

Social media can be huge, based on your church population. Use this tool strategically! Post recent pictures on the church's social media sites. Include short videos on Instagram and Facebook of the pastor introducing the church with a brief introduction and invitation. This is a perfect platform for posting important announcements, a new sermon series, or an invitation to a special event using professional graphics. There are many apps and sites to create excellent graphics, including a picture/video and some text. Many churches will create a video summary by the pastor to remind their members of a challenge or main points from Sunday and upload it to their social media. This helps keep the sermon fresh in their minds.

Some churches will assign one person to create a graphic or video montage on Sunday afternoon and share it as a reminder of earlier that day. Regular posts help keep church events in front of your members, allowing them to "like" and share within their spheres of influence. What a way for your church family to invite their friends next week! Start small, and do it well. Social media is powerful and is the place to share "life" with others, and that life should involve your church.

(START SMALL, AND DO IT WELL.)

Video is extremely effective in conveying information. Think of fifteen-or thirty-second commercials—essential advertising for companies. While not a for-profit company, churches ought to integrate video more regularly. Rather than hearing someone speaking with a microphone about how a group in the church helped renovate a home for a neighbor, imagine watching some clips with overlaid music. Then follow that with a live testimony of someone who served. Another church may use a graphic montage or video clips of how the church has served others before extending the invitation to give. Most people, including church members, want to know that their financial contributions are going to a good cause. Let's show them! How can you integrate videos into your service?

In addition, because our culture is often too impatient to read a whole article about a topic, they'll defer to a bite-sized excerpt. Enter tweeting. Twitter has become a platform to convey concise observations and insights with an occasional photo. Members of churches find that posting a memorable quote from the pastor's sermon provides a snapshot of Sunday morning to a broader audience. Of course, for those readers whose interest is piqued, they can follow a hyperlink to the recorded church service and/or website that is also posted. Digital marketing in today's culture cannot be overstated. It combines the call to "Go and tell" with "Come and see." We've gradually replaced the old paper handouts to invite our friends and neighbors to an event with modern communication not limited by proximity.

ADMINISTRATIVE COMMUNICATION

Always keeping in mind that people today prefer the ease of completing tasks from their smartphones, pastors and leaders can use this device for administrative purposes within the church service. Studies have found that providing an option for individuals to tithe from their phones increases the number of contributions received. Why? For many, it is more preferable to click a few buttons than to write a check or drop cash into a container.

I have seen Tithe.ly and Pushpay as two popular options. We live in a convenience culture. Passing the plate has slowly faded as the normal practice in many churches. But some congregations integrate all options—plate, phone, and giving kiosks—to appeal to varying audiences. As you can imagine, an older generation may just prefer to write a check every week, and that is okay. We want to meet people where they are while providing various methods to accomplish the goal.

Let's apply this concept to the means for attendees to respond in writing with a prayer request, praise report, or note for the pastoral staff. Connection cards were created for congregants to communicate for various reasons on a physical card, which they could drop off in the giving area or at a welcome center. What if you provided a way for people to communicate with the church leadership in other ways—perhaps from the convenience of their fingertips?

Some churches regularly display and refer to a specific number to text that pulls up information about the church: events, a link to tithe or to submit a prayer request or praise report, and opportunities to volunteer for an upcoming event. There are many options in the world of apps to implement this type of service. Again, it is another way for people to connect in a way convenient for them. Not only is a texting service helpful to convey information but also to receive information. While bulletins used to serve as the means of making announcements and sharing events, an e-bulletin could be accessed through texting or by providing a QR code that directs people to a website. The possibilities are endless.

MINISTRY TOOLS

How can you serve your congregation after they leave the church parking lot? Consider what would strengthen their spiritual growth—God's Word, worship songs, prayer, and fellowship. Could the use of technology assist in individual spiritual development? Absolutely! During the national shutdown in 2020, churches had to get creative and innovative to teach, encourage, and strengthen their members. In every state, online small groups assembled on Zoom meetings to see one another, read scripture, lead Bible studies, pray together, and provide needed support. Not only could we live stream sermons through Facebook pages and YouTube channels, but there was a chat feature that allowed people to write "Amen!" and "Preach it, Pastor!" from the comfort of their homes. It was pretty amazing to watch this "ministry platform" unfold and serve as a way to disciple people! Fast-forward to today—every week, thousands of churches stream their services that are then viewed by individuals in two hundred countries around the world. The gospel is getting out quicker than ever before. Praise the Lord!

CONSIDER WHAT WOULD STRENGTHEN THEIR SPIRITUAL GROWTH—GOD'S WORD, WORSHIP SONGS, PRAYER, AND FELLOWSHIP. COULD THE USE OF TECHNOLOGY ASSIST IN INDIVIDUAL SPIRITUAL DEVELOPMENT? ABSOLUTELY!

What is a worship service without music and singing? I love what some church leaders decided to do by creating worship set lists and distributing the URL links on social media platforms, YouTube, and music streaming apps, like Spotify, Apple Music, or YouTube music. Now you can find podcasts, sermon audio, and your church's favorite songs individually or as a group. Direct your church to search for certain set lists of five to twenty songs to play at home, work, or in between errands to lift your praise in worship. Let's use the available technology to disciple others! Give them the tools and allow them to build new godly habits.

One concept that is relatively untapped is a "tele-pastor." I know it sounds odd, but hear me out. What if a pastor was available to lead confidential, mini-counseling sessions for the hurting? Perhaps he could take questions about the Bible that he answers and records which later he can post online. Maybe a pastor or leader could lead a short Bible study or provide an explanation on how to have quiet time.

In essence, spiritual leaders make themselves available to meet with people remotely at scheduled times and provide teaching ministry for those not at church. Pastors are no longer limited by proximity and can use online video meetings for kingdom purposes. Small groups can even use a recorded message that you've prepared and direct it toward the unchurched friends of your church members. They could invite people over for lunch or dinner and watch your specially crafted message for that group, which then would lead to their discussion with preplanned questions. Let's think creatively to reach our church family and the lost for Christ!

FELLOWSHIP AND FUN

Not all great ministry ideas must involve digital technology! There is no replacement for in-person smiles, hugs, and fun. Let's make getting together more enjoyable with some intentional experiences. People love food. Why not have a coffee budget before or after service with snacks? Churches will sometimes announce that they've grilled hot dogs and hamburgers outside and invite everyone to stay to hang out.

Of course, music helps create a fun atmosphere before and after the worship service. Consider using a photo booth with a nice backdrop and some props. You know people love to take selfie and "friendsie" photos for memories! Assign individuals with an eye for creativity (and maybe a good quality camera) to discretely take photos each week of various experiences during rehearsal, the worship service, and fellowship time. These snapshots of the day are enjoyable to see later on social media, in a video montage, or in a slideshow.

SERVICE/VOLUNTEERS

In my travels, I have observed many churches and their ways of doing church life. One area of leadership that I believe all churches could improve upon is in the arena of volunteer relationships. The oil of the church is its volunteers, and they truly give a lot to make the church run smoothly. We need them! Too often, though, we forget that they are individuals with family responsibilities, work responsibilities, and home responsibilities; all of them could be somewhere other than serving at any given time. So we need to make much of them, and do it often! Celebrate these people every week. Speak words of encouragement and life into them privately and publicly because they are pouring out, and it can become draining.

THE OIL OF THE CHURCH IS ITS VOLUNTEERS, AND THEY TRULY GIVE A LOT TO MAKE THE CHURCH RUN SMOOTHLY. WE NEED THEM! SO MAKE MUCH OF THEM, AND DO IT OFTEN!

One church I know calls its volunteers the Dream Team. The church provides breakfast for them before they serve and showers them with recognition on Sunday mornings and beyond. This type of honor inspires others who are just taking up space to also get involved. You and your leaders can consider creating roles for new people to serve. Furthermore, invite one or two volunteers to share what serving has meant to them in front of the congregation or by video for the shy ones. New volunteers breathe fresh life into a group. Help make that happen!

NEXT STEPS

Let's finish off with how to transition people into the next stage of involvement. There should regularly be an invitation from the pastors to take the next step in their faith within the church. Because this step is often scary for many people, it should not be made difficult. After the service, don't instruct them to go down a hallway, take a right, then a left, and then descend a staircase. Have a clearly defined space for people to meet a hospitable leader who is friendly and knowledgeable of upcoming opportunities.

Many churches have prepared a "Meet the pastor," a short "New here" class, or "Journey" presentation at which leaders supply some food and a quiet atmosphere to hear about the church's vision, salvation, ministries, and ways to serve. Signing up should be quick and easy at a table or kiosk or by texting the church's designated number. People make judgments of events—for good or bad—based on the person they interact with. Be the one who emits excitement about how God is moving in your church and why you think that they should stick around to experience more. Your enthusiasm is contagious!

METHODS CHANGE IN MINISTRY, BUT THE GOSPEL DOES NOT CHANGE. I WANT TO CHALLENGE YOU TO EVALUATE YOUR COMMUNICATION, MARKETING, AND MINISTRIES. COULD THESE BECOME MORE ACCESSIBLE FOR YOUR OWN CHURCH MEMBERS?

Methods change in ministry, but the gospel does not change. I want to challenge you to evaluate your communication, marketing, and ministries. Could these become more accessible for your own church members? Are there methods you can change to meet people where they are? Don't get me wrong—our goal is never to water down God's truth. We are simply trying to build other bridges for our community to walk over, open up other lines of communication, and provide additional ways of connecting with us. These are some of the twenty-first century's new wineskins. We can use them as tools or to create relevance with a larger part of our population. Change is healthy!

CHAPTER 9

MARVEL TOGETHER: POWERFUL CELEBRATION

Throughout the Old Testament and the New Testament, we read of victories won by the Hebrew nation or by the newly birthed Christian community. Some victories came in battle; some were from the hundreds and thousands who came to faith in Christ through the gospel. Others involved signs and wonders done in the name of Jesus. There is something powerful when a group sets its focus on achieving a common goal. If you've ever participated in a team sport, you understand! We strategize as a group, pay close attention to the game, yell encouragement at teammates to prod them to give their all, clap at the success of someone's great performance, and finally, celebrate together with hollers and shouts at a win.

Have you ever wondered why present-day churches struggle to show that same exhilaration, passion, and joy when they gather? I'm sure you've heard of some groups of believers as "the frozen chosen." That's the last term that I want to be said about my church. No way! It got me thinking about why this happens in many churches. Is there not a reason to celebrate? Is there not joyful hope within their bones? Is there no victory to declare? On the contrary, there is much to celebrate!

WHATEVER THE REASONS, I BELIEVE THAT MOVING FORWARD REQUIRES SOME TIME TO MARVEL TOGETHER AT WHAT OUR KING HAS DONE, IS DOING, AND WILL DO.

In case you or your church family need a few reasons, allow me to list a few for you. Most importantly, God has forgiven every wicked sin of His followers and declared them innocent, holy, and adopted into His family forever. Celebrate! The King has assured glorious citizenship in His heaven that is beyond beauty and comprehension. Celebrate! In our hardest moments of life, His presence is our rest, deliverance, and hope because He is working all things for good on our behalf. Celebrate! Our good Father has constructed a body of believers called the church to be His physical representation on this planet to support and strengthen one another—a growing new family! Celebrate! And He has instilled in His people the Holy Spirit to lead, teach, empower, and encourage us in all seasons. Oh, celebrate with me, someone!

I'm only hitting on the highlights, Friend. We each have countless more reasons to praise Him independently and collectively. So why don't we do it more? Think about it for a second. Why don't you celebrate His victories in your life more often and with more joy? It is not because there aren't reasons to celebrate. It is not wrong to get excited in church. Perhaps, as Jesus explained in the parable of the sower, our life is being choked by life's worries, seeking wealth, and pursuing pleasures (Matthew 13:22). Maybe we've lost our focus on His work and victories. Whatever the reasons, I believe that moving forward requires some time to marvel together at what our King has done, is doing, and will do.

Looking back may be helpful at this point. Consider some "team" celebrations in the Old Testament. Do you recall the response of the Hebrew nation after they arrived on the other side of the Red Sea and watched the waters crash down on the Egyptian army? The writer says in Exodus 14:31-15:2 (BSB):

> When Israel saw the great power that the LORD had exercised over the Egyptians, the people feared the LORD and believed in Him and in His servant Moses. Then Moses and the Israelites sang this song to the LORD:"I will sing to the LORD, for He is highly exalted. The horse and rider. He has thrown into the sea. The LORD is my strength and my song, and He has become my salvation. He is my God, and I will praise Him, my father's God, and I will exalt Him."

All the people sang together. Then Miriam kept the celebration going, grabbed a timbrel, led the other women, and sang aloud for all to hear (Exodus 15:20-21).

At the dedication of the rebuilt wall in Jerusalem, Nehemiah and the families present who had returned from exile looked at their diligent effort finally finished and rejoiced. It was like a scene from an epic action movie—choirs standing on the wall and in the temple, priests blowing trumpets, all sorts of instruments being strummed and clanging, and people rejoicing: "On that day they offered great sacrifices, rejoicing because God had given them great joy. The women and children also rejoiced, so that the joy of Jerusalem was heard from afar" (Nehemiah 12:43, BSB).

Those are my kind of people! Can you sense their awe of God and His work as well as their elation at this group victory? He enabled a new season to begin in the life of the Jewish people by reclaiming the Promised Land after more than seventy years. Nothing could stop them from marveling and rejoicing together!

Consider team celebrations in the New Testament. Once Jesus ascended to heaven, His apostles "returned to Jerusalem with great joy. And they stayed continually at the temple, praising God" (Luke 24:52-52, NIV). Exhilarated by the reality of their Savior's presence, teaching, victory over death, and rising into heaven, they remained together to rejoice, commune, and pray. Fifty days later, at Pentecost, we find this small group still together praying in the upper room but now with about 120 people. There is power in rejoicing together when Christ is the central focus.

Once, Peter preached a sermon to thousands (Acts 2), and the church dramatically grew. Afterward, did they all just go their separate ways? No! In one accord, they met together every single day at the temple courts to receive the apostles' teaching, to pray, and for fellowship. This extended to joining each other in their homes to eat, celebrate communion, praise God, and pray (vv. 46-47).

God created His people for one another. Those who take God's Word and try to walk with His Spirit without communing with His people are missing a needed component of God's design for us. Even more, we don't just meet together, but we rejoice together, remembering His past promises, His present provisions, and His perfect palace above. There is much to celebrate about who He is and what He is doing!

And we must celebrate what is happening in our local church. Leaders ought to proclaim the spiritual growth of members through testimonies, successful outreach and service to the community, numerical growth and attendance in youth and children's ministries, money raised for various projects, and salvations. Find reasons to celebrate and make some noise for God's work among you.

AT SOME POINT IN THE FUTURE, WE WILL JOIN THE GREAT MULTITUDE AND REJOICE IN A WAY THAT WE HAVE NEVER BEFORE REJOICED.

Keep in mind that fullness of joy dwells in God's presence, and there is worshipful celebration continually before Him. We see a glimpse of this in what the apostle John wrote:

> And I heard a sound like the roar of a great multitude, like the rushing of many waters, and like a mighty rumbling of thunder, crying out: "Hallelujah! For the Lord our God the Almighty reigns. Let us rejoice and be glad and give Him the glory. For the marriage of the Lamb has come, and His bride has made herself ready. She was given clothing of fine linen, bright and pure." —Revelation 19:6-8 (BSB)

At some point in the future, we will join the great multitude and rejoice in a way that we have never before rejoiced. We will sing and loudly proclaim the glory of our King on His throne and His victories over His enemies. The question, then, is why we are not celebrating His victories here on earth more often. If sports teams have a temporal, less significant reason to yell, jump, and erupt, don't Christians have an even greater reason to do so? We have a good reason to celebrate!

How then do churches celebrate more? First, pastors should demonstrate a sincere spirit of gratitude to God when rejoicing from the platform, communicating to staff and volunteers, preaching sermons, and, whenever they can, testifying to God's greatness. Highlighting specific "wins" in and through the church body unifies the team. People see the vision implemented and success realized, and that is exciting. As in many arenas of leadership, pastors and directors must exemplify a spirit of celebration, turning everyone's focus to the King and His work.

Second, make a big deal of individual efforts and victories. While small progress is often overlooked by many, leaders can pay attention and recognize it publicly. Use a nicely assembled video and photo montage of recent events to convey successes. Many will not know until they are told, and some need to see it for themselves to believe it. How many new volunteers would be motivated to get involved and current leaders who are desperate for a little encouragement would be strengthened? Set aside time for testimonies of God's work among the church or small group. I heard it said that giving an old-fashioned witness is the lifeblood of the church. Why? People want to hear good news and see that

God still transforms lives. Leaders should be building testimonies into their agenda more often than they do.

TIMES OF CELEBRATION HAVE A PLACE AND PURPOSE, AND THEN WE OUGHT TO POINT RIGHT BACK TO THE MISSION BEFORE US.

Have you considered that communion and baptisms are celebratory? We quickly turn our thoughts to worshipful singing as the time to celebrate together and, yes, that is true. But we like to get loud and clap when Christians rise out of the waters of baptism. We celebrate their commitment to Christ, their salvation, their public declaration that they are on the winning side of eternity, and their step of obedience. Help people to understand the reasons to rejoice in this!

And when we eat and drink the elements of communion, indeed, there is a component of somber reflection at Christ's death, but what else does communion recognize? Jesus said to take the bread and cup in remembrance of Him, of His perfect redemption, of His unfathomable glory, of His sweet return, of His life within us. I view communion as a reason to rejoice privately and corporately. We ought to give thanks and praise to our Savior for giving us Himself and His trustworthy promises as we partake in communion.

As you know, there is a time for rejoicing together and a time to get to work. Churches must make celebrating a regular practice, remembering His goodness, His blessing, and His work in and through us. God's people, among all people, have reason to celebrate again and again, and they need perceptive leaders to identify and communicate these reasons. Yet, there is a time to get back to work, Friend. We are energized by our time of rejoicing together and then redirect our focus to the vision before us. Jesus reminded His disciples that the fields "are ripe for harvest" (John 4:35, NIV). Reflect on the past, and get ready for what still lies ahead. Times of celebration have a place and purpose, and then we ought to point right back to the mission before us. Recommitment follows rejoicing.

It's been said, "The family that prays together . . . stays together." I'll take some creative liberties and adapt that saying in light of what we just discussed: "Churches that celebrate well . . . live to tell!"

CHAPTER 10

MONUMENTAL INNOVATION: LEADING INTO THE FUTURE

"On that day a great persecution broke out against the church in Jerusalem, and all except the apostles were scattered throughout Judea and Samaria. . . . Those who had been scattered preached the word wherever they went."

—ACTS 8:1 AND 4 (NIV)

So, you've come this far in the book and likely have evaluated yourself, your ministry, and your future as a leader. Naturally, you've had some successes and a few failures along the way. Let's get two things clear: leading is difficult, and even the best leaders of organizations sometimes stumble in decision-making. Remember New Coke? It lasted for a whopping three months in 1985 before the entire product line was yanked from store shelves, and the classic formulation was returned. It was a massive fail . . . or was it? In a turn of events, consumers flocked to stores to mercilessly buy the tried-and-true classic product they loved. This insightful example reveals a few important observations about leadership:

- Even the best leaders make losing choices sometimes.
- Failures help us to develop.
- We can continue to innovate in spite of the past.
- The public can be very slow to change.

Do any of these statements ring true for you on your journey?

So, what causes some organizations and churches to fail? At the same time, what qualities and actions cause some to be incredibly successful? In this chapter, I want to unpack some answers to these questions, equipping you with knowledge and wisdom on how to lead change in the role that God has placed you in. As we work through the following pages, ask yourself, *What does it take to produce monumental change? Am I ready for what is demanded? How can I get more ready?*

IF HE HAS ARRANGED FOR YOU TO LEAD AT THIS TIME IN HISTORY, ACCEPT THAT YOU MAY BE THE ESTHER OF YOUR DAY FOR SUCH A TIME AS THIS.

Every season of change requires a leader who decides to take up the mantle to forge a pathway. In fact, there is personal development and preparation essential for the entire leadership team to help ensure a smooth transition of change within an organization. One problem is an overemphasis on managing instead of developing the quality of leadership that will create the "sacrifice, dedication, and creativity" that Gary Hamel of London Business School says we need for transformation.[11]

11 Gary Hamel, *Leading the Revolution* (Boston, MA: Harvard University Press, 2002).

The antithesis of a change mindset looks like the guy who stares at the daunting road ahead and says, "I've prayed about it, and the Lord isn't leading me. . . ." when, in fact, it was fear that discouraged him from proceeding rather than the Lord's voice. We must beware of speaking preemptively without truly spending time seeking the Lord, godly advisors, and a supportive team. Choosing to entertain the possibilities ahead requires self-reflection and courage. Be encouraged, though. If He has arranged for you to lead at this time in history, accept that you may be the Esther of your day for such a time as this. Where He leads you, His grace will sustain you.

At times, change is forced upon us when we or our churches face a fork in the road—a significant decision that must be chosen from among multiple options. Failure to act may result in stagnation, frustration, or even decline. It could be likened to riding a dead horse in hopes of someday arriving at your destination. No amount of strong leadership or creativity will motivate that dead horse to cross the finish line. Remaining stationary and being a change-denier is like riding that dead horse. When has the need for a prompt pivot of methods ever forced our hands?

Again, consider the national shutdown in 2020. Did church leaders desire to move their worship services online as their primary means of ministry for several months? No way! But did churches change their methods to accomplish the greater good of ministry, given the circumstances? Absolutely. The ones who refused to change significantly struggled to survive that season. Leaders during the shutdown who embraced online services stood a far better chance of making it through. Pivoting and changing directions is necessary to not just grow but survive in some cases.

When persecution broke out against the early followers of Christ in Jerusalem after Stephen's martyrdom, everyone except the apostles scattered. What the enemy meant for evil, God turned for good. The gospel spread throughout Judah, Samaria, Galilee, and beyond! Change was forced upon them, and they accepted the need to pivot, which required sacrifice but always reaped great fruitfulness. Recall that the gospel was once carried only by foot, then by letter, then by horseback, then by automobile and train, and then via the internet. Using new and creative means to achieve the greater ends in ministry—salvation, discipleship, community, and service—is like taking the gospel from horseback to a 5G network.

MONUMENTAL INNOVATION WILL LEAD TO SIGNIFICANT GROWTH AND INVOLVE NEW MODELS THAT TRANSCEND PRESENT MODELS AND SYSTEMS.

I'd like to expand on four wise "I" principles of leading change: innovation, integration, incubation, and implementation. Gary Hamel, one of the world's foremost thinkers on management and business strategy, wrote an excellent piece on how to successfully navigate change. In *Leading the Revolution*, he distinguishes between innovation and methodology. So that we're all on the same page, the introduction of the smartphone was innovation, as there was a shift from a device that only made phone calls to one that had Wi-Fi capabilities—a significant leap in functionality and purpose. That dramatic move was not a simple upgrade of features, as between one Apple iPhone and the next year's model. Uber also broke the mold by using individuals' personal cars, GPS tracking, and a revolutionary system to change the personal transportation industry. That is innovation!

One could compare it to the difference between macroevolution (from one species to an entirely new species) and microevolution (adaptations within a species). Apple iPhones are adapting year to year, so to speak, while a horse-and-buggy evolving into the modern automobile falls under the macro or innovative change.

Hamel uses the concept of adding a third, fourth, or fifth blade to a razor not as innovation but as an adaptation of the same model. People assume innovation equals new products when, in fact, they are extensions of the original. Monumental innovation will lead to significant growth and involve new models that transcend present models and systems.

THE INNOVATIVE LEADER LOOKS AT THE CORE ISSUES FACING AN INDUSTRY OR FIELD AND CONSTRUCTS MODELS TO EVALUATE CURRENT TRENDS AND BE AT THE CUSP OF FUTURE ONES.

What some pastors do is look at what other pastors across the road or across the country have done and attempt to replicate it in their own organizations. The innovative leader looks at the core issues facing an industry or field and constructs models to evaluate current trends and be at the cusp of future ones. Others' packaged ideas, however, may not be right for another geographic region or population. Hamel points out, "Few senior leaders have a clear, well-developed model of what innovation looks like as an organizational capability. And since they do not know what it looks like, they do not know how to build it."[12] Thankfully, we have numerous models to consider, helping us to develop a deeper understanding of what innovation looks like in our church and community.

One prime example of innovation in the world of Christianity involves moving from the printed Bible to a digital page on Bible apps like YouVersion. The pages of the Bible now live on a microchip within your device or in cyberspace and can be accessed instantaneously throughout the world. Accessibility and delivery of the Scriptures completely changed with the genesis (no pun intended) of these apps. World-renown businessman and innovator, Elon Musk, took a staple product, the automobile, and transformed a part of

12 Gary Hamel, *Leading the Revolution.*

it—the engine—to revolutionize the industry. We have successfully shifted from gas-powered vehicles to electric vehicles (EV). Moreover, the public now has access to self-driving automobiles. Innovation upon innovation and more to come, I'm sure.

In the church world, the use of video messages was innovative in the early 2000s. Craig Groeschel, pastor of Life.Church, now a multisite, nationwide church network, stumbled upon this idea when preparing to be away one Sunday from his one-site church building. To be present for his child's birth, he instructed his team to videotape his sermon during the week to be played in his absence. His church family loved it. What began as a secondary plan snowballed over time to a new system to show the prerecorded video at another campus location, which then evolved to live streaming it to multiple locations as Wi-Fi functionality expanded. Innovation occurred because a need or a crisis demanded it. Now millions of people are hearing the gospel and maturing in their faith. This is the power of innovative change from outside the box thinking.

PASSING A CLEAR VISION AND PLANS TO THE ENTIRE CHURCH BODY ACTS AS YEAST IN DOUGH, SYSTEMATICALLY AND ORGANICALLY INTEGRATING AND EXPANDING, CREATING A RICHER IDENTITY TOGETHER UNDER A NEW MISSION.

The next "I" stands for *integration.* For change to occur in churches, the pastor states the goal, explains why change is needed, casts a vision to a strategic "change team" of leaders, and develops a plan with them. Leading this core group to believe in and invest in this collective sense of destiny holds enormous weight during this stage, empowering them to dream of unconventional strategies and uncover "deep capabilities." This is "a term used to indicate where a company's competitiveness resided not just in acquiring the capabilities to do something, but on making the capability a central part of their purpose."[13] Integrating the vision for something grander swells within this smaller group, inspiring these members to become primary catalysts of thought generation and change.

This vision and plan then must move through the whole church body. It is all-hands-on-deck to see this through. Talk about it often. Passing a clear vision and plans to the entire church body acts as yeast in dough, systematically and organically integrating and expanding, creating a richer identity together under a new mission. Rather than an autocratic style of leadership, often expressed as, "Thus saith the Lord, 'You all must follow my lead,'" wise leaders allow the idea to circulate, permitting discussion and explanation, working through concerns with the whole group, problem-solving with the vision in mind. The key is to build firm trust with the church body at this critical time so that they willingly invest their hearts and minds in the coming work.

Consider how you would integrate new families into a church. They initially are on the peripheral, looking in. The goal is to move them gradually toward the center of involvement and investment—Next Steps meetings, classes, small groups, volunteering, leadership, etc. As is human nature, some will run toward that center while others will meander and get there eventually. What conditions facilitate this process? You want to provide more and more exposure through various means of communication to convey the heart of your church, showing pictures and videos of your church family, the worship experience, serving together, and other events.

Churches use creative teams and social media, emails, phone calls, texts, and letters to keep the idea of their church in front of them. Integration takes strategic effort by the leadership team with resources of time, people, funds, technology, and supplies. Your change team coalition drives the thinking process of these plans as only one person will not consider every issue. The team

13 Gary Hamel, *Leading the Revolution.*

is essential, and a secure leader understands that integration of a plan involves more than just him or her.

Third, change requires a phase of *incubation*. Like sowing seeds into cultivated soil and providing regular nourishment, a vision takes time to root and grow. Change needs to become part of the DNA of a church, and that takes time. When leaders let a vision incubate, they give it time to breathe, allowing the whole group to become increasingly accustomed to the idea of something new.

It reminds me of a great illustration of one pastor who came into the role with ideas of his own. One idea involved moving the old organ from one side of the platform to another place on the platform. When he advocated for and insisted on this change, the church deacons fired him. The next pastor came. He also believed that the organ should be moved but chose a different approach to change. Learning from his impatient predecessor's mistakes, the new pastor moved the organ one inch every week until it finally arrived at the desired location. The story is both humorous, sad, and insightful.

ALL THE WHILE, PEOPLE ARE WATCHING YOU, AS WELL AS THE LEADERSHIP TEAM, FOR DIRECTION, EXAMPLE, AND HOPE THAT THE CONGREGATION WILL SURVIVE THE SEASON OF CHANGE.

Gradual acceptance can be the key to gaining group support. People should not be rushed to acceptance too quickly. A guiding coalition of team members waters and feeds the vision, vibrantly conveying plans and the changes to come. This phase requires patience in leaders since people embrace change at differing rates. Consider changes over the years in churches that ruffled many feathers: hymns to praise-and-worship songs, hymnals to screens on the wall, pews to theater seating, choir robes to casual clothes, pastor's suit and tie to business casual and very casual. Wise leaders let their people have sufficient time to breathe in these changes and exhale. They inwardly knew that the change would come, and they were given a season to mentally prepare for it. Such is wise leadership. Such is the benefit of incubation.

The final "I" is *implementation*, which pertains to enacting the components of a change event—the speed of the rollout, how it is communicated, the frequency of its mentioning, how leaders model change through attitudes and practice, and handling challenges. Thus far, the leader has built a strong coalition team, laid out the vision, and given it time to take root in the minds and hearts of the people. The preparatory work is done—the soil is cultivated. Now begins the work of doing the change. Buildings start to break ground, renovations take place, products are rolled out to the public, sponsorship letters are mailed, and staff members are hired. Action has begun, and this is an exciting time.

As you implement, be aware of obvious and subtle obstacles; take steps to remove them. These involve having serious conversations with resistant members to alleviate concerns, helping them see the purpose of the change, and encouraging them to support it. It involves evaluating what is going well and what is not, learning from successes and mistakes, and adapting methods without deviating from the vision. Implementation involves building momentum and excitement by identifying those who have made changes happen along way and recognizing their efforts. Repeat those success stories to different groups. Under the same umbrella, be sure to celebrate small victories as you hit important markers. Negativity will undoubtedly arise as the process wears on, which can discourage the team and process, so celebrate short-term wins often. Every step forward should be tied back to the vision and why you are walking through a season of forward-thinking change.

Preparing for growth takes time, thoughtfulness, and sacrifice from everyone. Just like expectant parents get a nursery ready over several months, so leaders must do the same on a grander scale. Old processes and structures will get in the way at times. Let your team discuss these and put in place the structures needed for change. Additionally, staff and roles may need to be adjusted to support the vision. Budget line items will expand or contract. Being a change agent requires fortitude and courage, especially when asking others to traverse the land of the great unknown for the greater good.

All the while, people are watching you, as well as the leadership team, for direction, example, and hope that the congregation will survive the season of change. This stresses the importance of one's own attitude and focus on both the Savior and end goal. The writer of Hebrews conveys this concept by reminding his readers to "fix [their] eyes on Jesus" (Hebrews 12:2, BSB). As in all change, we rely on the stability of our Savior and assurance of His leading to find personal comfort and hope. Such an attitude exemplifies to the entire group how to plod through transitions, discomfort, and sacrifice with grace and faith.

(IN ALL CHANGE, WE RELY ON THE STABILITY OF OUR SAVIOR AND ASSURANCE OF HIS LEADING TO FIND PERSONAL COMFORT AND HOPE. SUCH AN ATTITUDE EXEMPLIFIES TO THE ENTIRE GROUP HOW TO PLOD THROUGH TRANSITIONS, DISCOMFORT, AND SACRIFICE WITH GRACE AND FAITH.)

Consider the wisdom of Jesus. With only three and a half years to establish the church, He laid a foundation and ensured the continuance of the church by investing in ordinary men who caught the vision and became extraordinary leaders. Perhaps the greatest deficit the church is facing today is a leadership deficit. You are currently in the unique place you sit now because of the providence of God for the purpose of God with the people of God. You are there for such a time as this. Change begins with one person. Be that person who listens to God and obeys His leading at the expense of what is comfortable and normal. Your family, church, community, and beyond need you to shepard them through the change process.

Monumental innovation involves more than simply changing methods. Ministers and ministries married to their method more than their mission will meet their demise. Read that again. Pastors and leaders in the Christian community must look forward not just to this year but to the years to come. What battles will we face as a Christian community? How can we provide support, ministry, and leadership for our changing culture and local population? Let's get ahead of the curve and allow ourselves and our teams to think deeply and dream richly. Seek the Lord's guidance, along with that of gifted leaders, in your planning. There is wisdom in much counsel. Finally, forge ahead and blaze a trail to fulfill Jesus's Great Commission to go and make disciples. (See Matthew 28:19.) For the sake of God's ever-expanding kingdom, embrace change and boldly follow the mission He has prepared for you . . . the mission that leads outside the box!